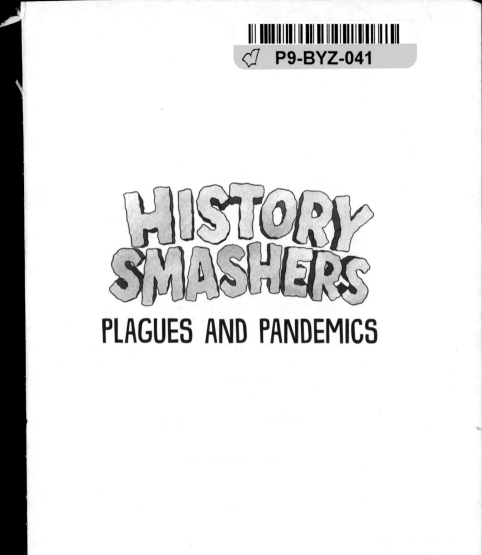

HISTORY SMASHERS

PLAGUES AND PANDEMICS

THE HISTORY SMASHERS SERIES

The Mayflower

Women's Right to Vote

Pearl Harbor

The Titanic

The American Revolution

Plagues and Pandemics

PLAGUES AND PANDEMICS

KATE MESSNER

ILLUSTRATED BY FALYNN KOCH

With special thanks to Ella Messner, who served as a researcher and contributor for this book

RANDOM HOUSE 🏠 NEW YORK

Text copyright © 2021 by Kate Messner
Cover art copyright © 2021 by Dylan Meconis
Interior illustrations copyright © 2021 by Falynn Koch

Visit us on the Web! rhcbooks.com

Educators and librarians, for a variety of teaching tools,
visit us at RHTeachersLibrarians.com

Library of Congress Cataloging-in-Publication Data
Names: Messner, Kate, author. | Koch, Falynn, illustrator.
Title: Plagues and pandemics / Kate Messner; illustrated by Falynn Koch.
Description: First edition. | New York: Random House Children's Books, [2021] |
Series: History smashers | Includes bibliographical references and index.
Identifiers: LCCN 2021005414 | ISBN 978-0-593-12040-8 (trade pbk.) |
ISBN 978-0-593-12041-5 (lib. bdg.) | ISBN 978-0-593-12042-2 (ebook)
Subjects: LCSH: Epidemics—History—Juvenile literature. | Plague—History—
Juvenile literature. | Diseases and history—Juvenile literature. | Communicable
diseases—History—Juvenile literature. | Black Death—Juvenile literature. |
COVID-19—Juvenile literature.
Classification: LCC RA653.5 .M47 2021 | DDC 614.4/9—dc23

Printed in the United States of America
10 9 8 7 6 5 4 3
First Edition

For Sandy, Bill, and Evelyn

CONTENTS

You've probably heard about the Black Death and other big disease outbreaks in history. If you're reading this book, you've probably even lived through one yourself.

Widespread outbreaks of illnesses make history because they can alter populations, power structures, and government policies. They've taught us about science and changed the way we deal with everything from throwing away garbage to preventing disease and caring for the sick.

But some of the stories told about outbreaks are just plain wrong. A long time ago, people were certain that diseases were caused by angry gods or bad-smelling air. If you were sick, friends might advise you to drink wine or eat crushed emeralds. If those cures didn't work, you might have tried putting pig bladders full of hot water under your armpits!

Thankfully, most of those way-off-base remedies are a thing of the past. Today, we know that many diseases are caused by tiny organisms known as microbes, such as bacteria and viruses. And today, most people—but not all—listen to science instead of myths when it comes to understanding illnesses and treatments. Still, the history of plagues and pandemics is full of stories that need smashing, starting with ancient times and continuing through today. So let's get to work. . . .

ONE
ANCIENT AILMENTS

Microbes have been around a lot longer than people, and they'll probably be around well after we're gone. Most microbes are harmless or beneficial. They help us digest food and fight off infection. But microbes can also make us sick.

When lots of people get sick from the same microbe at the same time, that's called an epidemic.

When an epidemic spreads around the world, it's called a pandemic.

The first recorded epidemics in history go all the way back to ancient times. *The Epic of Gilgamesh,* a poem written in ancient Mesopotamia, mentioned a visit from the god of pestilence (disease) around 2000 BCE. Ancient Egyptian and Chinese writings also refer to pestilence.

One of the first well-documented epidemics was the Plague of Athens, which happened in 430 BCE. The Greek city-state of Athens was fighting Sparta in the Peloponnesian War, and Athens had built walls around the city. People from the countryside moved inside to be protected, creating a super-crowded place where disease could spread easily.

A general and historian named Thucydides wrote that a quarter of the Athenian army died. What made them sick? We don't know, because people didn't understand diseases well at that time, but we can make some guesses based on ancient writings.

Fortunately, Thucydides himself got sick! While this was rotten news for him, it was good news for modern scientists and historians who have tried to piece together what happened in Athens. These are the symptoms Thucydides wrote down:

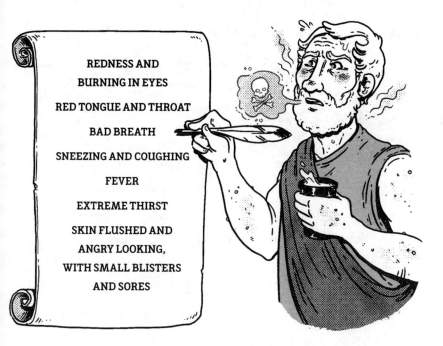

REDNESS AND
BURNING IN EYES

RED TONGUE AND THROAT

BAD BREATH

SNEEZING AND COUGHING

FEVER

EXTREME THIRST

SKIN FLUSHED AND
ANGRY LOOKING,
WITH SMALL BLISTERS
AND SORES

"Internally it burned so that the patient could not bear to have on him clothing or linen even of the very lightest description; or indeed to be otherwise than stark naked. What they would have liked best would have been to throw themselves into cold water, as indeed was done by some of the neglected sick, who plunged into the rain-tanks in their agonies of unquenchable thirst."

—THUCYDIDES, *HISTORY OF THE PELOPONNESIAN WAR*

Based on the list of symptoms, modern-day experts think the disease might have been smallpox or measles. Even though it's called the Plague of Athens, they don't think it's likely that people had bubonic plague, because that disease produces big bulges on the body, called buboes, which would have been hard for old Thucydides to ignore in his descriptions. Whatever it was, the epidemic devastated Athens, which lost the war. It was the beginning of the end for what had been the most powerful city-state in Greece . . . all because of a microbe, a tiny germ that no one could even see.

THE MUMMIES HAD MALARIA

Some of ancient Egypt's disease history is recorded in the bodies of preserved mummies. Around 6000 BCE, when people started farming in Egypt, they noticed that the Nile River flooded once a year, swamping the valley on both sides. The flooding was great for creating fertile soil for crops, but it was also perfect for mosquitoes, which breed in standing, shallow water. Mosquitoes can carry a tiny parasite that causes a disease we now call malaria.

In 1922, archaeologist Howard Carter opened the inner shrine of the tomb of King Tutankhamen, better known as King Tut. Scientists now believe the king had malaria before he died at age nineteen.

Papyrus scrolls written by doctors in ancient Egypt talk about "the pest of the year," an illness that showed up when the river flooded. Was it malaria? Thousands of years later, some well-preserved mummies still held the answer to that question. Archaeologists studied a group of mummies from one area of Egypt and found that almost half of them showed evidence of being infected with malaria.

The more people travel, the more diseases can spread. As ancient trade routes opened up, microbes hitched a ride on ships and caravans carrying silk and spices. And when armies traveled during wartime, their crowded camps were a perfect breeding ground for bacteria and viruses.

Back then people didn't know what was making them sick. The ancient Greeks blamed angry gods and believed that if you were ill, you needed to patch things up with the gods so they'd make you well again. So they built asclepeions, which were sort of half shrines and half hospitals where sick people could go to ask priests for help with cures. Asclepeions were located in pretty country settings with clean air and pure water, and people who went there were encouraged to eat a healthy diet, exercise, and get lots of rest. Those practices were probably why some of the sick got better—not because the priests there had some sort of direct line to the gods.

If you think being treated at an asclepeion sounds pretty great, there's one more thing you should know: one of the cures involved having snakes slither over you. The snakes were considered sacred and could supposedly make people well . . . somehow.

The tradition came about because Asclepius, the god of medicine and healing, was often pictured with a serpent curled around his staff. This snake imagery is still connected to medicine today; both the American Medical Association (AMA) and the World Health Organization (WHO) have serpents on their logos.

Later on in ancient Greece, people wondered if something other than angry gods might be making people sick. A philosopher named Aristotle suggested that the world was made up of four elements—earth, water, air, and fire. He and his students also thought the human body contained four fluids called humors—black bile, phlegm, blood, and yellow bile—and if these humors got out of balance somehow, they made a person sick.

That explanation wasn't quite right, of course, and it led to some questionable treatments. If doctors thought you had too much blood, they'd just slice you open with a sharp tool called a lancet to get rid of some. This treatment, called bloodletting, persisted for thousands of years. In fact, America's first president, George Washington, was bled right before he died in 1799. He'd come down with a fever, and doctors thought bleeding him might help. (Spoiler: It didn't.)

Even though the ancient Greeks got a lot wrong, the idea that diseases were caused by something natural was a starting place. Once doctors understood that, they could test different theories to learn more.

THE FATHER OF MEDICINE

World's Best Dad (of Medicine)

Hippocrates, who lived from about 460 to 377 BCE, was an ancient Greek doctor who came to be known as the father of medicine. The information he recorded about his patients helps us document diseases that existed in ancient Greece. He wrote about a mumps outbreak on the island of Thasos. In other patients, he described symptoms that modern experts believe were probably tied to cases of malaria, diphtheria, tuberculosis, and influenza.

Hippocrates had some questions about that theory that the four humors caused illness. For one thing, he noticed that sometimes a whole lot of people in one place got sick at the same time. It seemed super weird that they'd all have the exact same sort of imbalance at once. But perhaps there was another cause. Could the illness be related to where people lived? Maybe they were all inhaling bad air from a big bunch of decaying matter in a swamp.

Hippocrates and his followers came to believe that disease was caused by miasma, some sort of bad vapors in the air. Maybe that bad air came from decaying corpses or something rotten in the earth. Whatever caused it, that bad air was making people sick . . . somehow. (There were a lot of "somehows" in ancient people's ideas about disease.)

Hippocrates's idea about bad air wasn't much better than angry gods or unbalanced humors as an explanation for disease, but once in a while it led to some lucky solutions. Doctors back then didn't know that mosquitoes carried malaria. They thought cases of the disease were related to the time of year and proximity to water. But that *did* lead ancient Romans to drain some of the swamps. And it worked! Not because it got rid of the "bad air" around the murky waters, but because it reduced the breeding grounds for the mosquitoes that spread the disease.

ALEXANDER THE GREAT VS. TYPHOID THE EVEN GREATER

You've probably heard of Alexander the Great, a Greek king who lived from 356 to 323 BCE. He's one of history's most famous military commanders, so you're probably imagining that he died in a big dramatic battle somewhere. But he didn't. He got wiped out by a microbe.

An ancient Roman mosaic of Alexander the Great

Alexander and his troops managed to conquer the whole Persian Empire. But after sailing down the Euphrates River, he developed a fever. Two weeks later he was dead. Today, scientists and historians understand that he probably picked up a microbe while he was traveling though the marshlands along the river. Ancient records say his fever lasted eleven days, which makes modern scientists think that typhoid fever, an infection caused by bacteria in contaminated food or water, may have been to blame.

SO, WHAT MAKES US SICK?

Bacteria and viruses cause many diseases that make people sick. What's the difference between those two kinds of microbes?

Bacteria are living things. Scientists first observed them under a microscope in the 1600s. They're single-celled organisms that can reproduce on their own under certain conditions. While most are harmless or even helpful, some can make us sick. Different kinds of bacteria cause illnesses such as strep throat and some types of food poisoning.

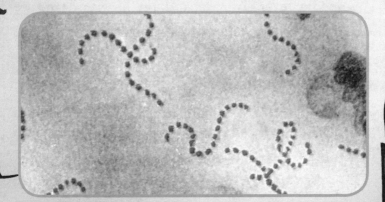

Streptococcus pyogenes, the bacterium that causes strep throat, as seen under a microscope at 900x magnification

16

Viruses are a little harder to explain. They don't meet the criteria to be considered living things, since they can't reproduce on their own. A virus is a bit of DNA or RNA, which are both kinds of genetic material, inside a coat made of protein molecules. Viruses can't multiply unless they get inside a living cell—like one of yours. When a virus gets inside your body, it uses your cells to make copies of itself; that's how it reproduces and makes you sick. Viruses cause illnesses like common colds, chicken pox, influenza, and

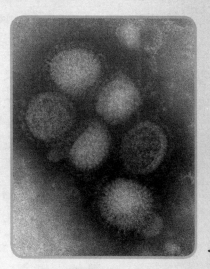

The H1N1 influenza, or swine flu, virus, as seen with an electron microscope

COVID-19. Viruses are a lot smaller than bacteria, so people couldn't see them until better microscopes were invented in the 1900s.

Microbes can spread in a number of different ways. Sometimes they're transmitted through contaminated food or water. That is most common with microbes that cause stomachaches and diarrhea. This is a huge problem in places where people don't have access to clean drinking water.

Some microbes spread through droplets. When we're sick with a cold or the flu and we sneeze or cough or even talk, we send out tiny drops of spit that contain the virus. When other people breathe in those particles or touch something contaminated and then touch their nose or mouth or eyes, they can become infected, too.

Some microbes only spread directly from person to person via bodily fluids. That's the case with both Ebola virus and HIV (human immunodeficiency virus), the virus that can lead to the disease AIDS (acquired immunodeficiency virus). And some microbes are transmitted to people by other living creatures. Malaria and yellow fever spread this way, through certain kinds of mosquitoes.

MICROBE MATH

Why do some microbes spread more quickly than others? Why do some spark pandemics, while others fizzle out? The answer to those questions has to do with microbe math.

Microbes need hosts to infect. They spread most easily when lots of people are in close contact with one another. Once an epidemic begins, it tends to continue as long as plenty of hosts are around to infect.

There's an important number that epidemiologists, or disease doctors, talk about with epidemics. It's called R0, pronounced "R-naught," and it represents the number of new infections on average that come from each person infected within a population. In other words, it's an estimate of how many people each infected person will pass the infection to. The R0 value for a disease tells us how infectious it is.

If a disease's R0 number is greater than one, then the epidemic keeps chugging along and spreading. But when it drops to less than one, the epidemic begins to die out. This number often gives scientists clues as to how long an epidemic might last.

TWO

THE BLACK DEATH

The Black Death is probably the most famous pandemic in history. Nearly everyone has heard of the bubonic plague outbreak that swept through Europe starting in 1347, leaving a trail of death and terror. But few people realize that this was just one of many outbreaks of the disease caused by a bacterium called *Yersinia pestis,* which is still around today.

To get to the bottom of the Black Death, we have to go way back in history, to the days of ancient Rome. No one called it bubonic plague then, but historians believe that's what caused the epidemic known as the Justinian

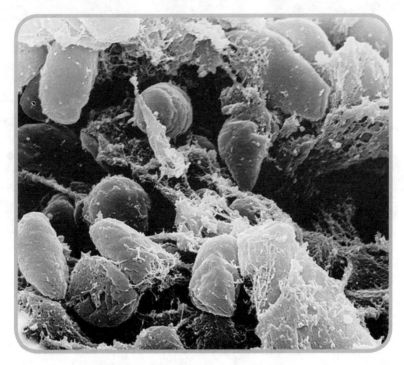

Yersinia pestis bacteria, as seen with an electron microscope

Plague (named for the Byzantine emperor at the time), which broke out in 541 CE. Modern experts estimate that 20 million to 50 million people died in the outbreak as it spread—about half of the world's population back then. Some people wore name tags when they went outside, so they could be identified later if they fell sick in the streets. A scholar named Procopius, who lived through the plague, wrote about how awful it was.

> *During these times, there was a pestilence by which the whole human race came near to being annihilated.*

Some people in Justinian's day were still stuck on the angry-gods idea. They said that Justinian was a crummy emperor, so the gods were making everybody sick to punish him. But thanks to Procopius, we know it was good old *Yersinia pestis*. Procopius described the symptoms people had, including the one that's unique to bubonic plague—buboes, or bulges, in the armpit or behind the ears, where people's lymph nodes are. This was likely the first epidemic of bubonic plague in Europe. It continued on and off for two hundred years, then vanished for six hundred years and showed up later as the Black Death.

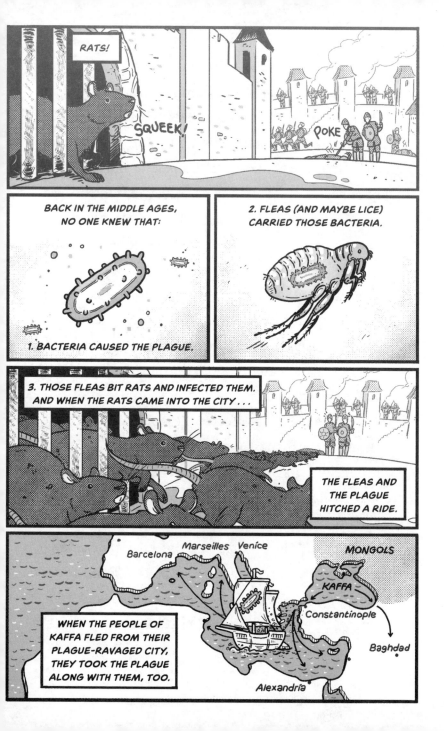

Medieval Europe was pretty gross. There were no toilets, so waste was dumped into the streets. People rarely took baths because they thought bathing would open their pores and make them sick. (If you're thinking that medieval Europe must have been a pretty stinky place, you're right!)

Most people were infested with lice, and their homes were full of mice and rats. When plague-infected fleas bit those rats and made them sick, the rats died, and the fleas needed new hosts, so they jumped to people and bit them. And here's the really gross part.

(You may want to skip the next paragraph if you're eating lunch.)

When a plague-infected flea bit someone, that flea didn't just suck up some blood and move along. It puked up its stomach contents into the person it was biting. That meant someone could be infected with up to twenty-five thousand bacteria from a single fleabite. When people were infected, the bacteria grew silently in their bodies for up to a week. Then, according to Michael of Piazza, a Franciscan friar who wrote about the disease, blisters would appear.

At first these were of the size of a hazelnut and the patient was seized by violent shivering fits, which soon rendered him so weak that he could no longer stand upright, but was forced to lie on his bed, consumed by a violent fever and overcome by great tribulation. Soon the boils grew to the size of a walnut, then to that of a hen's egg or a goose's egg, and they were exceedingly painful.

The sickness typically lasted three days, and on the fourth, most patients died. It was terrifying, so people came up with all kinds of ideas for how to prevent it. Someone heard that people who drank wine didn't get the plague, so there was a run on wine. Others tried to ward off the plague by eating eggs, fruits, and vegetables (which probably helped with general health, at least) or crushed emeralds (which didn't).

Remember that idea that miasma in the air caused illness? That led some people to shut all their windows and doors, which must have made the bad smells in those stuffy medieval houses even worse. Others wore vials of herbs and spices around their necks so they could sniff those scents all day instead of breathing in the bad air. This tradition led to images of plague doctors dressed up in elaborate outfits that made them look like they couldn't quite decide what they wanted to be for Halloween—the Grim Reaper or a weird, creepy seagull. The plague doctor is one of the most famous symbols of the Black Death, but it turns out that this is one of those stories that needs to be smashed.

The truth is, these images of costumed plague doctors with beaks full of herbs to fight off the disease weren't even around during the Black Death in the fourteenth century. They didn't show up until centuries later, when there was another outbreak in Europe. And there's no evidence that most doctors who treated plague patients then dressed like that. There may have been a few (and you can see why they got so much attention!), but the rest just dressed like regular doctors, so that well-known plague doctor outfit is more myth than reality.

This myth about the plague is harmless, but others aren't. Often, when people don't understand something that scares them, they look for someone to blame. During the Black Death, officials rounded up foreigners and Jewish people, who were then driven out of cities, beaten, and even killed. On Valentine's Day 1349, Christians at Strasbourg in Alsace accused two thousand Jewish people of poisoning the wells where people got their water. The Jewish people were told they had to convert to Christianity or face punishment. Half promised to give up their religion. The other half were killed. And then the city passed a law that said no Jewish people could enter. Antisemitism, or prejudice against Jewish people, wasn't new, even then. But the fear surrounding the plague gave people an excuse to act on their feelings of hate.

What was causing the illness? No one knew, but people came up with all sorts of wild ideas. Scholars from the University of Paris told the king of France it was related to "the configuration of the heavens" because Saturn, Mars, and Jupiter were lined up. People thought a recent lunar eclipse might have had something to do with the illness, too. Somehow.

Another guy, Henry Knighton, wrote a whole book about his ideas on the plague. He blamed it on a bunch of women who were running around dressed like men and performing at tournaments.

Henry Knighton was upset because these women were doing all sorts of manly things like spending money and holding weapons, not to mention wearing pants. According to Henry, God was obviously angry about this and sent the plague as punishment.

Okay, Henry.

The good news is, some of the medieval people's wrong ideas about the plague eventually led to one pretty smart idea about how people can prevent disease—quarantine.

Quarantines are periods of isolation designed to stop the spread of disease, and they're still used in public health today. During the Black Death, people didn't understand microbes, but they saw that this disease was spreading, so they sealed off towns with the plague. And when ships arrived at a port, they were isolated for forty days.

THE FIRST MEDICAL REFERENCE BOOK

Medieval doctors struggling to understand the plague were still working with the same old ideas Hippocrates had put forth more than a thousand years earlier in ancient Greece, but they also had another helpful book, written by a Muslim doctor named Abu Ali al-Husayn Ibn Sina, who lived from about 980 to 1037 CE. In the West, he was called Avicenna, and he created the world's first comprehensive medical reference. It outlined a new system for training doctors and caring for patients.

A fourteenth-century drawing of Avicenna

Avicenna had memorized the Koran, Islam's sacred book, by the time he was ten years old. He began studying medicine at age thirteen and was treating patients three years later. His *Canon of Medicine,* about medical theory, disease, and treatments, contains over one million words. Avicenna didn't get everything right, but some of his ideas are still in practice. He advised doctors to remove malignancies, or cancerous tumors, by surgery, which is still done today. And Avicenna's ideas about how to test new drugs laid the groundwork for modern-day clinical trials, the large-scale tests that are used to approve new treatments for everything from cancer to COVID-19.

The Black Death pandemic lasted from 1347 to 1352, and even after that, the disease kept resurfacing. Smaller epidemics popped up around the world, and people began sharing new ideas about how the disease might spread.

A sixteenth-century Italian doctor named Girolamo Fracastoro was among the first to suggest that something other than unbalanced humors or bad air was at work. He wondered if there was some kind of poison

Girolamo Fracastoro that could spread from person to person. He didn't know what it might be, but he was drifting toward the idea of germs and how they work.

In the seventeenth century, a German named Athanasius Kircher took the theory a step further, saying the plague was spread by something he called "animalcules," which were transmitted from infected patients to healthy people. He was getting even closer!

Athanasius Kircher

In 1665, London was hit with another big plague outbreak that killed about a quarter of its population. The plague came to France and Italy in the 1700s, and then it seemed to simply vanish for more than a hundred years. It showed up again in China in 1855 and Hong Kong in 1894 and then spread around the world via international trade routes.

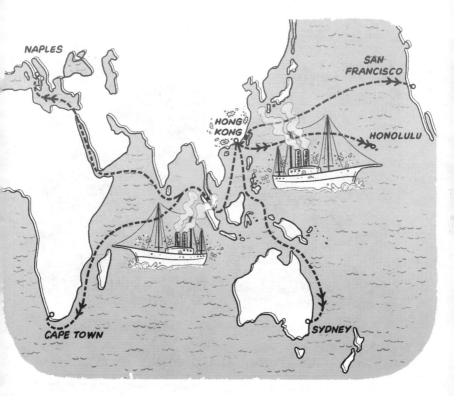

During this outbreak, seven thousand people died in Europe and another five hundred in the United States. But developing nations were hit much harder. As many as thirteen million to fifteen million people died in India between 1898 and 1910. It was during this third plague epidemic that scientists finally figured out what was going on. Two researchers—one Swiss-French and one Japanese—rushed to Hong Kong to study plague patients.

Alexandre Yersin

Shibasaburo Kitasato

Alexandre Yersin and Shibasaburo Kitasato didn't collaborate on their research; they were rivals in a race to see who could find answers first. Yersin even bribed his way into the morgue so he could get samples from plague victims. By then, people had learned a bit about microbes. (We'll talk more about how in chapter 6.) He ended up being the first scientist to describe the plague bacterium, so it was named after him. (He's the Yersin in *Yersinia pestis*.) A few years after the bacterium was identified, a French scientist named Paul-Louis Simond figured out that rats and fleas were the carriers. This led communities to get rid of rats as a way to deal with the disease. Medicines called antibiotics, which kill bacteria, were developed later on.

THE STORIES OLD BONES TELL

When the plague swept through London in the seventeenth century, some of the dead ended up in mass burial pits. Hundreds of years later, archaeologists found some of those pits, and scientists have been studying old bones to learn new things about the plague. For starters, they were able to confirm that *Yersinia pestis* was the culprit. Researchers sampled DNA in teeth from plague victims and identified bacteria in victims' remains.

Plague victims were often buried in mass graves like this one in France, 1720–1721.

Another group of scientists studied mortality, or death, data from nine cities affected by the plague. They used modern mathematics to create models of how the illness might have spread. The researchers discovered that rats and rat fleas probably weren't the only culprits. It's likely that fleas and lice that lived on people and their clothes were spreading the disease, too.

We like to think of bubonic plague as a disease of the past, but that scrappy old *Yersinia pestis* is still around today. Bubonic plague was introduced to the United States during that outbreak around 1900, and it's still carried by ground squirrels and other rodents in western states. According to the Centers for Disease Control and Prevention (CDC), an average of seven people a year come down with the plague in the United States. Most are hunters or campers who come in contact with one of those wild rodents and their fleas.

So why don't we hear about deadly plague out-breaks on the news? Scientists who have studied the DNA of *Yersinia pestis* say it hasn't changed much since the days of the Black Death. But now we have antibiotics to treat people who get the plague, so it isn't the killer it used to be, and most of those people survive.

THREE
THE SCOURGE OF SMALLPOX

If the plague tops the list of most feared diseases in history, smallpox might be a close second. A person who was infected with the smallpox virus would first notice a fever, headache, and muscle aches. On about the third day, spots would show up in the mouth, throat, and nose. A day or two later, a skin rash appeared—first red spots, then fluid-filled lesions, or blister-like sores, that hardened and caused terrible pain. After about two weeks, the sores scabbed over, and a week or so later, the scabs fell off, frequently leaving deep scars. And that's how it went for the *lucky* ones. Smallpox killed about one in every three people who caught it. The good news is that survivors had immunity, which meant they wouldn't catch the disease again.

HOW IMMUNITY WORKS

Your body fights off harmful microbes in a whole bunch of ways. First, your skin and the mucus in your nose help keep germs from entering your body.

When microbes do make it inside, your immune system kicks in to fight that specific invader. Your body produces antibodies—special proteins that attach themselves to specific parts on the surface of microbes so they can be killed or weakened.

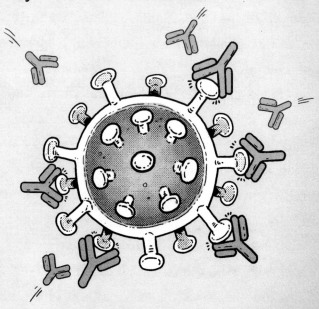

Usually, it takes a little while for your immune system to fire up and start making antibodies. But often, after your body has been infected with a microbe once, your immune system "remembers" it, so you can fight off the germ right away if it shows up again, usually before you even get sick. That's what it means to have immunity.

Vaccines trigger the same immune response without actually making people sick. They trick the body into thinking it's been attacked by a microbe, and the body produces an immune response. Then when the real microbe shows up, the person is already protected.

Some antibodies stick around longer than others, so immunity doesn't always last forever. That's why some vaccines require boosters, or later doses. And some viruses and bacteria are quick to mutate, or change, which makes things tricky. The virus that causes influenza acts this way, so scientists have to develop a new flu shot each year. HIV, the virus that can lead to AIDS, also mutates, which is one reason it's been so difficult to develop a vaccine.

Most kids in the United States get about ten vaccines between birth and ten years of age. Chances are, the antibodies you developed after receiving those vaccines are protecting you from a bunch of diseases right now.

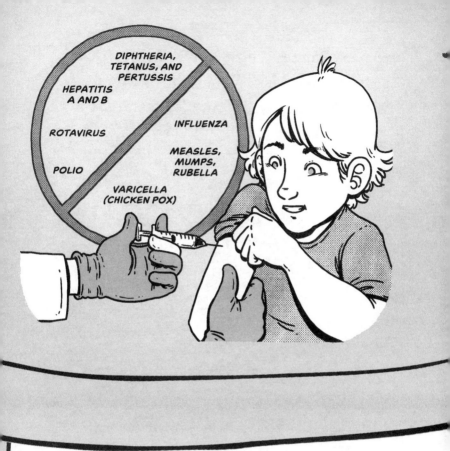

Based on writings from ancient scholars and historians, we know the first recorded smallpox outbreaks happened more than three thousand years ago. Sanskrit medical texts from ancient India describe a disease that sounds a lot like smallpox, going all the way back to 1500 BCE. And scientists are pretty sure smallpox killed the Egyptian pharaoh Ramses V in 1157 BCE. When archaeologists discovered his mummified remains, his face and neck were covered in pustules, those fluid-filled spots that are a telltale sign of the virus.

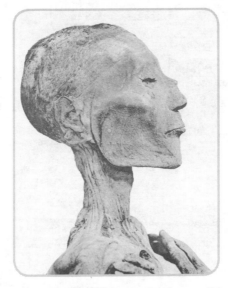

The mummified head of Ramses V

By the year 1000 CE, there had been smallpox outbreaks all over Asia. Armies spread the disease through Africa and Europe. And then explorers brought it to the Americas, where it devastated Native people. To understand why that happened, you need to know a little history, a little geography, and a little science. First, the geography and history . . .

About fourteen thousand years ago, during the Ice Age, there was a land bridge between the places that are now called Siberia and Alaska. That changed when sea levels rose at the end of the Ice Age. With the land bridge gone, people who had crossed it into North America over thousands of years were cut off from Europe and Asia—and from their microbes.

Before European explorers arrived, as many as 112 million Native people lived in what we call the Americas. They included the Incas in what is now Peru, the Aztecs in what's now central Mexico, and the Taino people who lived on the islands where Christopher Columbus landed, now called the Bahamas. For thousands of years, they had hunted wild game, cared for their families, run their communities, and made art.

When European explorers showed up with their guns and germs, Native people had no built-up immunity or resistance, unlike the people who'd been exposed to the microbes when they were kids growing up in Europe. So when diseases began to spread, Native people died by the millions. That made it a lot easier for European explorers, including Columbus, Francisco Pizarro, and Hernán Cortés, to steal their land and natural resources and enslave the Native people who survived.

Wherever European explorers and colonists arrived, they brought disease with them. The Pilgrims, who settled in what is now Massachusetts in 1620, noticed that they never seemed to get sick, even as Native people were dying around them. They didn't know about immunity, and that made it easy for them to believe that God was on their side. John Winthrop, the governor of the Massachusetts Bay Colony, even suggested that God had sent smallpox to make life easier for him.

The good hand of God favoured our beginning ... in sweeping away the great multitudes of the Natives by the Small Pox.

Later, the British weren't willing to wait for God to spread smallpox anymore. They decided to do it themselves, making a microbe into a weapon. Sir Jeffery

Amherst was the commander of British troops in North America in 1763. At that time, the British were fighting Ottawa, Wyandot, Ojibwa, and Potawatomi people in what's come to be known as Pontiac's War.

"Could it not be contrived to send the smallpox among those disaffected tribes of Indians? We must, on this occasion, use every stratagem in our power to reduce them."

—BRITISH COMMANDER
JEFFERY AMHERST

"I will try to innoculate the Indians by way of blankets that may fall in their hands and take care however not to get the disease myself."

—BRITISH COLONEL
HENRY BOUQUET

That June, William Trent, a trader at Fort Pitt, wrote in his journal that he'd given infected linens to two men from the Delaware tribe who had visited the fort. "We gave them two Blankets and an Handkerchief out of the Small Pox Hospital. I hope it will have the desired effect." There's no historical evidence to suggest that this plan was successful in making anyone sick, so the plot didn't seem to have much of an impact on the war.

Smallpox *did* play a big role in the American Revolution, though, when the colonists fought for freedom from Great Britain. The disease devastated American troops until they were inoculated, which means they were infected with a mild case of smallpox on purpose so they'd be immune to the disease after that. This idea of *using* the virus to teach the immune system to *defeat* the virus would eventually lead to the development of many vaccines that keep us healthy today. You might be surprised to know people were thinking about this way back in the 1700s, but the truth is, the concept of inoculation goes back even farther than that.

People in ancient China used to crush dried smallpox scabs into a powder to inhale. Sniffing scab dust might not be your idea of a healthy lifestyle, but it worked. People often came down with a milder form of smallpox and then had the protection of immunity. The technique spread to India, Persia, and Turkey. Sometimes instead of inhaling, people scratched a person's arm with a needle and rubbed fluid from a smallpox pustule into the scratch. It was around 1700 when the Royal Society of London, a group of scientists and scholars, heard about this ancient tradition and started collecting data on it.

Lady Mary Montagu, whose husband was the British ambassador to Turkey, saw the procedure there and decided to have her son variolated, or inoculated. She also told her wealthy friends about this method of protecting people from bad cases of smallpox, and the idea caught on. The practice spread to America at a time when Washington's army was losing more men to disease than to Redcoat bullets.

George Washington on horseback at the
Battle of Princeton, 1777

"Finding the Smallpox to be spreading much and fearing that no precaution can prevent it from running through the whole of our Army, I have determined that the troops shall be inoculated. This Expedient may be attended with some inconveniences and some disadvantages, but yet I trust, in its consequences will have the most happy effects."

—GEORGE WASHINGTON

Those "inconveniences" and "disadvantages" were a big deal. Inoculation carried real risk. It was supposed to infect people with a very mild case of smallpox, but about 2 percent of those people died. That was a big improvement over the death rate for people who caught the disease during an outbreak, though. Once Washington had his soldiers inoculated, smallpox became less of a problem in the Continental Army. After the war ended, scientists came up with a safer way to protect people from the virus.

THE BIG BREAKTHROUGH WITH SMALLPOX CAME FROM A COUNTRY DOCTOR NAMED EDWARD JENNER.

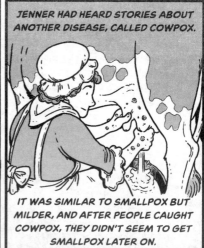

JENNER HAD HEARD STORIES ABOUT ANOTHER DISEASE, CALLED COWPOX.

IT WAS SIMILAR TO SMALLPOX BUT MILDER, AND AFTER PEOPLE CAUGHT COWPOX, THEY DIDN'T SEEM TO GET SMALLPOX LATER ON.

JENNER WONDERED ABOUT THIS, SO IN 1796, HE PLANNED AN EXPERIMENT. HE TOOK SOME FLUID FROM A COWPOX PATIENT . . .

BUT THE TRUTH IS, EDWARD JENNER WASN'T THE FIRST TO EXPERIMENT WITH COWPOX. TWENTY YEARS BEFORE HIS FAMOUS EXPERIMENT, AN ENGLISH FARMER NAMED BENJAMIN JESTY TOOK SOME FLUID FROM A COWPOX LESION ON ONE OF HIS COWS AND USED IT TO VACCINATE HIS WIFE AND SONS. JESTY HAD NOTICED THAT SERVANTS WHO HAD COWPOX DIDN'T SEEM TO GET SMALLPOX, EVEN WHEN THEY WERE EXPOSED TO IT.

BUT JESTY WAS A FARMER—NOT A SCIENTIST OR DOCTOR—SO HIS WORK WASN'T SHARED AT THE TIME, AND JENNER'S NAME IS THE ONE THAT BECAME FAMOUS.

Jenner went to the Royal Society in London, ready to share what he'd learned with the world. But the Royal Society pretty much told him to get lost. The group refused to publish his experiment and said he should shut up about his "wild idea" if he valued his reputation. Jenner ignored the advice, did more experiments, and self-published a pamphlet with his findings.

That pamphlet got attention. Some people were intrigued and hopeful about Jenner's vaccine. Others were totally against it, even if it meant protecting people from a deadly disease. These anti-vaccine people made up outlandish stories. They said that it was unnatural to take something from cows and inject it into humans, claiming that vaccination would result in . . . well . . . weird things happening. One guy suggested Jenner's vaccine might result in the ladies of Britain running out to canoodle with bulls in the fields.

Seriously. Someone said that. His name was Benjamin Mosely, and he was a doctor who was involved in traditional inoculations that used the real smallpox virus, so he was going to stop making so much money if Jenner's cowpox vaccine replaced it.

The Cow Pock — or — the Wonderful Effects of the New Inoculation! — vide the Publications of ye Anti Vaccine Society

"The Cow-Pock—or—the Wonderful Effects of the New Inoculation!" was an anti-vaccine cartoon that showed Jenner vaccinating people, who then began to sprout cow horns and, inexplicably, little cow faces popping out of their bodies in various places.

In spite of the vaccine opponents, Jenner's vaccine gained popularity, and he realized it might end up wiping out a disease that had plagued the world for centuries. In 1801, Jenner wrote, "The annihilation of the smallpox, the most dreadful scourge of the human species, must be the final result of this practice."

That didn't happen right away. People still got smallpox, including American president Abraham Lincoln, who got sick not long after he gave his famous Gettysburg Address during the Civil War. Lincoln developed a headache and a fever on his train ride home, and a couple of days later, the telltale rash showed up. Lincoln had a mild case, though, and reportedly even made a joke about having a contagious disease when so many people came to him looking for jobs and other favors.

Jenner was long gone by the time the world reached his goal of taking out smallpox once and for all. By then, a more modern vaccine had replaced Jenner's cowpox version. With advances in science and a global campaign that began in 1959, a huge worldwide vaccination effort finally eradicated, or got rid of, smallpox. It's the only time in history an entire human disease has been wiped off the face of the earth.

HEALTH CARE HEROES

One of the health care heroes behind the global smallpox effort was Donald Henderson, an Ohio doctor who joined the World Health Organization, a team of international experts committed to improving public health all over the world.

Donald Henderson

Henderson's job was to head up the WHO's smallpox eradication program in 1966. He led the WHO in its goal to vaccinate the world against smallpox and reduce cases to zero by reporting and containing any outbreaks along the way. The last documented case was recorded in Somalia in 1977, and three years later, the WHO declared success.

Today, the smallpox virus exists only in laboratories. Just two labs in the world are approved to have samples for research—the Centers for Disease Control and Prevention in Atlanta, and the Russian State Center for Research on Virology and Biotechnology. Because smallpox is no longer a threat in the world, it's not on the list of vaccines you probably had when you were a baby or before you started school. But there are still doses of the vaccine around. The United States keeps the Strategic National Stockpile, with lots of different kinds of medicines and medical supplies. It includes enough smallpox vaccinations for everyone in the country to have a dose, just in case the disease ever returns.

FOUR
FEVER AND MOSQUITOES

As smallpox swept through the Americas, another virus crossed the Atlantic. Yellow fever began with a headache, chills, and fatigue. Many patients felt better in a few days, but then the virus often hit back hard, with symptoms that were downright horrific.

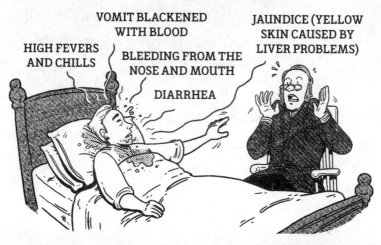

VOMIT BLACKENED WITH BLOOD

JAUNDICE (YELLOW SKIN CAUSED BY LIVER PROBLEMS)

HIGH FEVERS AND CHILLS

BLEEDING FROM THE NOSE AND MOUTH

DIARRHEA

The first recorded case of yellow fever in the Americas happened in Barbados in 1647. By then, most of the Native people who lived in the region had died of other diseases, and plantation owners were bringing enslaved African people to replace them in the sugarcane fields. When enslavers packed those captive people onto ships to cross the Atlantic, yellow

fever came along, too. No one knew it at the time, but this microbe is carried by certain species of mosquitoes. Some mosquitoes of the species *Aedes aegypti* likely hitched a ride on a ship, breeding in water barrels and water that pooled in cracks in the hold.

When slave ships arrived in the Americas, infected crew members and enslaved people came ashore, and so did mosquitoes. Once a female mosquito bites a yellow fever patient during the right stage of the disease, she's infected and can inject the virus into a new victim every few days, as often as she feeds.

As the slave trade grew, yellow fever spread through the colonies. The virus created problems for British troops during the American Revolution. When the Redcoat army headed south in 1780, commanders were faced with an impossible choice: keep the army inland, where it was cut off from supplies brought by ship, or move it to the coast, where soldiers kept catching diseases. They didn't know that mosquitoes were the problem; they just noticed they all got sick when they hung out near the swamps.

In 1793, yellow fever broke out in Philadelphia, which was America's largest city and temporary capital at the time. Ships sailed in frequently from the West Indies that summer; people were fleeing slave rebellions that resulted from terrible working conditions on sugarcane plantations. Refugees who arrived in Philadelphia told stories of a fever that had been spreading through the islands. In mid-August, Philadelphia doctor Benjamin Rush noticed increased sickness in the area. When he learned that a bunch of rotten coffee had been dumped on the wharf after a voyage from the West Indies, he felt sure he'd found the culprit.

Rush convinced the mayor to clean up the water-front, and soon the stinky rotten coffee was gone. But the yellow fever stuck around. The city tried setting up a quarantine to keep ships from unloading immediately when they arrived, but that didn't help. (Have you ever tried to quarantine a mosquito?) Half the population of Philadelphia fled town. Newspapers offered all kinds of shady advice about how to avoid the disease.

DIFFUSE TOBACCO!

SPRINKLE VINEGAR AROUND THE HOUSE!

LIGHT A BONFIRE OUTSIDE TO PURIFY THE AIR!

PUT A ROPE IN YOUR ROOM! NO, WAIT. . . .

CARRY THE ROPE IN YOUR POCKET!

BOOM!

FIRE THE CANNONS!

Rush, who'd been wrong about the rotten coffee causing the disease, was sure he was right about what could cure it—bleeding patients to get rid of "bad blood." Other doctors in town argued that the practice just made people sicker and weaker. But they didn't have any better ideas, so Rush kept at it with his lancet. He also gave people drugs to make them throw up, which he thought would help them.

The deaths continued into September, and by then the city had a huge problem. No one wanted to care for the sick or bury the dead. So Rush went to leaders of Philadelphia's Black community to ask if they'd take on the job. That's probably no surprise to you if you know anything at all about how Black people were treated in colonial America. Pennsylvania was in the process of abolishing slavery, but even free Black people weren't allowed to hold many kinds of jobs. They were often given work that no one else wanted to do. And burying yellow fever victims totally fell into that category.

There was also a belief—a wrong one—that Black people couldn't get yellow fever. That may have been true for many of those who were brought from Africa and had immunity from being exposed as children, but it wasn't the case for most people born in the Americas. Still, Rush promised Philadelphia's Black residents they weren't likely to get sick and strongly encouraged them to step up and help out. Many agreed to do just that.

Absalom Jones

Richard Allen

Absalom Jones and Richard Allen organized the effort. They ran the Free African Society, a group they'd founded in 1787. It was one of the first organizations for Black people in America.

The Free African Society historical marker in Philadelphia

JONES AND ALLEN TOLD THE REAL STORY OF HOW THEY WERE TREATED.

"WE SET OUT TO SEE WHERE WE COULD BE USEFUL. THE FIRST WE VISITED WAS A MAN IN EMSLEY'S ALLEY, WHO WAS DYING, AND HIS WIFE LAY DEAD AT THE TIME IN THE HOUSE, THERE WERE NONE TO ASSIST BUT TWO POOR HELPLESS CHILDREN. WE ADMINISTERED WHAT RELIEF WE COULD, AND APPLIED TO THE OVERSEERS OF THE POOR TO HAVE THE WOMAN BURIED."

JONES AND ALLEN WROTE ABOUT ANOTHER BLACK MAN WHO WENT FROM HOUSE TO HOUSE HELPING PEOPLE WITHOUT EVER GETTING PAID.

WHEN THAT BLACK VOLUNTEER GOT SICK AND DIED, WHEN HIS FAMILY NEEDED HELP, PHILADELPHIA'S WHITE RESIDENTS WERE NOWHERE TO BE FOUND.

THE PAMPHLET ENDED WITH AN OLD PROVERB:

God and a soldier, all men do adore,

In time of war, and not before;

When the war is over, and all things righted;

God is forgotten, and the soldier slighted.

The epidemic raged through September and October, killing five thousand people before it finally began to fade away after the weather turned cold. It disappeared at about the same time as—you guessed it—the mosquitoes. But there would be many more outbreaks before people made that connection.

Yellow fever returned to the United States again and again. When it hit New York City in 1798, the deaths were so frequent that boys were selling coffins in the streets. Yellow fever was also raging through the Caribbean again. There, it helped a Haitian general named Toussaint Louverture change the course of history.

Toussaint Louverture

By 1800, Toussaint had led a slave uprising on Hispaniola and become governor-general of the whole island. Slavery had been abolished, but the part of the island called Saint-Domingue (now Haiti) was still a French colony. And French military leader Napoléon Bonaparte wanted to enslave people again. So Napoléon sent an army of soldiers across the ocean. He planned to crush Toussaint's revolt, bring slavery back to the island, and from there move on to establish a whole French empire in North America.

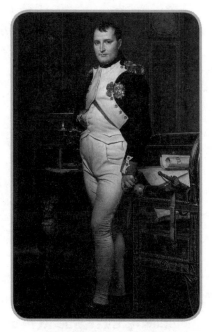

Napoléon Bonaparte

But Napoléon underestimated the challenge he faced—not just from Toussaint's soldiers but also from disease. Yellow fever raced through the French army, but many of Toussaint's Black troops had immunity. Toussaint was counting on that. He lured French troops into ports and lowlands, knowing that when the rainy season arrived, so did yellow fever. He even wrote to his second-in-command, Jean-Jacques Dessalines, urging him to keep fighting until the rains came.

Do not forget that while waiting for the rainy season, which will rid us of our enemies, we have only destruction and fire as our weapons.

French troops died by the thousands, and in late fall of 1803, those who were still alive gave up, piled onto their ships, and went home. Toussaint had been captured and died in a French fort, but Dessalines declared independence and named the new country Haiti.

This is another situation where a microbe probably changed the course of history. Because things went so poorly for him on Hispaniola, Napoléon decided his plans for a North American empire might not be such a good idea after all. Many historians believe that the French leader's defeat at the hands of Toussaint, Dessalines, and yellow fever led him to sell the Louisiana Territory to the United States.

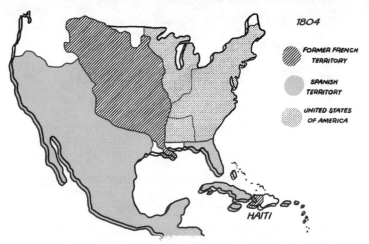

Neither France nor the United States acknowledged that the land included in the Louisiana Purchase didn't really belong to either of them; it was, and is, the traditional territory of the Caddo, Choctaw, Sioux, Pawnee, and other Native people from dozens of different nations. Much of that land hadn't even been colonized yet, so really it wasn't *land* that the United States was buying. It was the right to buy or steal that land from Native people without France getting in the way.

Yellow fever outbreaks continued in the United States through the 1800s. An epidemic killed more than eight thousand people in New Orleans in 1853. When the disease spread through Memphis in 1878, people fled the city, just as they'd hightailed it out of Philadelphia in 1793.

THE YELLOW FEVER PLOT

A New Orleans man was arrested for conspiracy to commit murder after he reportedly tried to bring back that old germs-in-the-blankets trick. Luke Blackburn supported the Confederacy (made up of Southern states) in the Civil War, fighting against the United States. He was a doctor and treated yellow fever patients during an 1864 outbreak in Bermuda. When some of his patients died, he was accused of collecting their bedclothes, packing them in trunks, and sending them north, hoping they'd start an outbreak so the Confederacy could win the war.

Blackburn was eventually caught and stood trial, but he was acquitted, or found not guilty, because the evidence against him wasn't solid enough, and some of the witnesses were apparently pretty shady characters themselves. Blackburn tried to rebuild his reputation by treating patients in that Memphis yellow fever outbreak of 1878. Apparently that worked out for him, because he was elected governor of Kentucky in 1879.

Luke Blackburn

The ironic thing about this whole conspiracy is that none of it mattered. Even if Blackburn *had* been able to sell those bedclothes to Northerners, that's not how yellow fever spreads. It's transmitted by mosquitoes and can't be spread the way smallpox can, when a person inhales droplets of virus-containing spit—or dust from a germy blanket.

Yellow fever shaped history again when it halted work on the Panama Canal, a waterway designed to connect the Atlantic and Pacific Oceans. Work on the canal had started in 1881, with workers chopping a path across Panama, in hot, rainy Central America. But before long, two hundred workers a month were dying of yellow fever and malaria. Work slowed, and in 1888, the company building the canal couldn't raise any more money. The project stalled for a few years until the United States, under President Theodore Roosevelt, took over.

A political cartoon from 1905 illustrated the huge challenge yellow fever posed for the Panama Canal.

Yellow fever was still a threat, but scientists were finally beginning to understand what caused it.

HEALTH CARE HEROES

Carlos Finlay

No one knew what was really causing yellow fever until 1881, when a Cuban doctor named Carlos Finlay suggested that the disease was transmitted by mosquitoes. He even identified the species—*Aedes aegypti*—and recommended controlling mosquito populations as a way to stop yellow fever from spreading. Nineteen years later, a US Army doctor named Walter Reed led a team to Cuba to confirm Finlay's theory with more research.

THE YELLOW FEVER TEAM

Walter Reed

James Carroll

Jesse Lazear

Aristides Agramonte

The men arrived in Cuba in 1900 and began
their research, hoping to prove once and for
all that mosquitoes transmitted yellow fever.
You wouldn't have wanted to be a volunteer

in their lab. The job involved being bitten by mosquitoes right after those mosquitoes had feasted on blood from yellow fever patients!

But people actually signed up for that, including American doctor Jesse Lazear, who was bitten by an infected mosquito and died of yellow fever.

After that happened, the team members reported that mosquitoes were definitely transmitting the virus. You might think a dead researcher would be pretty compelling proof, but not everyone believed them. The *Washington Post* called the idea "silly." So Reed and his team did more research.

They were helped by William Gorgas, the chief sanitary officer in Havana, who launched a program to get rid of the city's mosquitoes. And guess what? As soon as the mosquitoes disappeared, so did the yellow fever. (Bonus! Wiping out the mosquitoes also got rid of malaria, which is transmitted by another kind of mosquito.) The discovery that mosquitoes transmitted those diseases was big news for the Panama Canal project. Steps were taken to disturb mosquito breeding grounds, which eventually allowed the canal to be finished in 1914.

Getting rid of mosquitoes was really the only way to prevent yellow fever until 1937. That's when Max Theiler, a scientist with the Rockefeller Foundation, developed a vaccine. He won the Nobel Prize in Physiology or Medicine for his work.

Max Theiler

Yellow fever hasn't caused an outbreak in

the United States in a long time, but it's still a problem in parts of Africa and South America, killing about thirty thousand people each year. The World Health Organization launched a major vaccine effort in 2009 to help protect people in areas where yellow fever is common. Despite this effort, cases of yellow fever have increased in recent years. Scientists say the increase is largely due to deforestation (cutting down trees) and climate change, which creates more of the warm, wet weather that mosquitoes love.

DID YOU KNOW . . . ?

Only female mosquitoes bite. They can drink up to three times their body weight in blood in a single feeding.

FIVE
KING
CHOLERA

Remember all those wild ideas people used to have about what causes disease? The theories about angry gods and bad air took a long time to die out, but by the late 1800s, scientists were onto the real culprit—germs. Two deadly diseases caused by bacteria—cholera and tuberculosis—led the way to some of those discoveries.

Cholera is passed from person to person through oral-fecal contamination. That's a nicer way of saying it spreads when someone eats food or drinks water that's contaminated with poop (and the bacteria in it). If those bacteria make it to the person's small intestine, they reproduce, and then the immune system starts fighting back. Usually, that's a good thing, but as cholera bacteria die, they release a toxin, or poison, that causes extreme diarrhea.

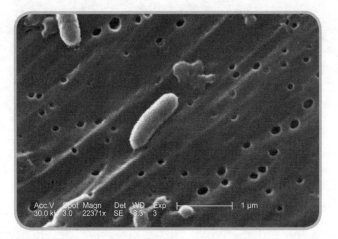

The *Vibrio cholerae* bacterium, as seen with a scanning electron microscope (at 22,371x magnification!)

During cholera outbreaks, patients often became sick very quickly, and many died in public. That's helpful to historians. Like bubonic plague, cholera was disgusting and memorable, so people wrote about it, leaving us records about when and where the disease struck.

But for the people who lived through those outbreaks, it was terrifying. Cholera was pretty much the scariest disease of the nineteenth century. Nearly half of those who were infected died. As if that's not scary enough, the disease could make people's muscles contract after they died—so cholera victims would twitch and shake in the death carts that rolled down the streets. Can you imagine how creepy that must have been? People gave the disease nicknames, calling it King Cholera or the Monster.

Cholera really took off when more people began to travel. Railroads, steamships, and the Suez Canal, which connects the Mediterranean Sea with the Red

Sea, all helped it along. An epidemic that began in Asia in 1826 spread to Europe and then jumped to Canada on a ship full of passengers from Ireland. Cholera broke out in the United States from 1852 to 1859 and in South America in the 1880s.

To understand the spread of cholera, you need to know that things were different back then when it came to getting rid of waste. Today, most people in developed nations go to the bathroom in toilets. When that waste is flushed away, it goes to a treatment plant, where it's broken down and disinfected before anything is released into the environment. But that didn't happen back in the 1800s, so most rivers and other waterways ended up contaminated with untreated sewage—and all the microbes that go with it.

You've probably heard over and over that washing your hands well is one good way to avoid getting sick. That's always been true. But even today, not everyone in the world has access to clean water. During the cholera outbreaks of the 1800s and 1900s, people who didn't have safe housing and clean water were a lot more likely to be infected with cholera. Major outbreaks in cities could bring five hundred deaths in a day.

Back then, people thought cholera was spreading in the air . . . somehow. (Those darn miasmas again!) It wasn't until 1854 that anyone caught on about the contaminated water. That year, a doctor named John Snow was paying close attention to an outbreak in London

John Snow

and began to suspect that people were catching cholera from their drinking water. He started making maps to keep track of how the disease was spreading through London.

Before long, Snow figured out that people who got their water downstream from where sewage was

dumped into the river were *nine times* as likely to get cholera as those farther upstream. One neighborhood that got its water from the Broad Street Pump was especially hard hit. Snow convinced officials to take the handle off that pump so it couldn't be used anymore. When that happened, there were suddenly way fewer cases of cholera. Unfortunately, Snow died before he could figure out exactly what was in the water that was making people sick. And a lot of people simply ignored his ideas about contaminated water anyway, so the outbreaks continued.

CONSPIRACY THEORIES AND CHAOS

Because cholera hit poor people harder than wealthy people with access to clean water, it highlighted the difference in privilege between social classes. Poor people wondered why doctors and city officials could spend time in their neighborhoods treating patients and enforcing laws without getting sick themselves. It was because doctors and others who visited those neighborhoods didn't drink the water, which was spreading the disease. But residents didn't know that, and they grew suspicious. Was the whole epidemic some kind of plot against poor people? Could the upper class be poisoning them somehow? This distrust of the government and wealthy people sometimes sparked violence.

Cholera outbreaks in cities during this time led to changes in how people got rid of sewage and supplied clean drinking water. They also led scientists to make groundbreaking discoveries. A German doctor named Robert Koch found that people who died of cholera seemed to have the same sort of comma-shaped bacteria in their guts. That was *Vibrio cholerae.*

Robert Koch

A vaccine for cholera was developed in the 1880s, but it was expensive and didn't offer protection that lasted long enough to be truly effective. Death rates dropped when doctors figured out they could treat cholera patients by hydrating them—providing fluids to replace those lost when they were sick. But the world hasn't managed to get rid of this disease. It still kills tens of thousands of people globally each year. The real solution to cholera and other diseases that spread this way will come when everyone has reliable access to clean drinking water. But that goal is a long way off. The World Health Organization estimates that at least 2 billion people around the world are without safe, clean water.

VACCINES: NOT JUST FOR VIRUSES!

Because many common vaccines protect against viruses, it's not unusual for people to assume that vaccines *only* offer protection against viruses and don't work against bacteria. But that's a myth that needs smashing!

Vaccines have been developed for both viral and bacterial infections. Of the twenty-six vaccinations used in the United States today, ten are for illnesses caused by bacteria.

There *are* medicines called antibiotics that work only on bacteria and not on viruses. That might be one reason that people get confused and think vaccines are just for viruses. But vaccines aren't really about killing microbes; they're about firing up the immune system, which is why they can work for both.

SIX

TUBERCULOSIS . . . AND NEW IDEAS ABOUT GERMS

Before he discovered the bacterium that causes cholera, Robert Koch was busy doing research on tuberculosis, which was rampant in the eighteenth and nineteenth centuries, during the Industrial Revolution. That's when people started working in factories and living in poor, crowded neighborhoods nearby, which made it easy for the microbe to spread.

Tuberculosis is caused by microbes that become airborne when infected people cough or breathe. But most people don't get sick right away. When the bacteria reach a healthy person's lungs, their immune system attacks the invading microbes to contain them. But the bacteria don't go away. They hang out and wait until the person's immune system is weakened in some other way, perhaps by a different infection or poor nutrition. Then the infected person gets sick, starting with a dry, hacking cough that's worse at night. In later stages, patients have severe respiratory problems, muscle loss, sunken cheeks, hollow eyes, and deathly-pale skin. The disease was sometimes called consumption because patients looked as if they were wasting away.

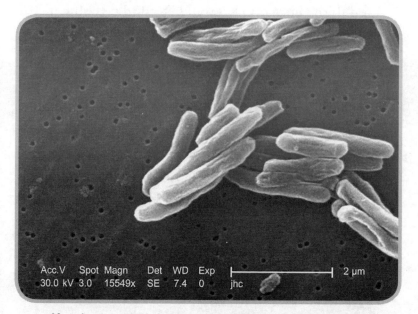

Mycobacterium tuberculosis, as seen with a scanning electron microscope (at 15,549x magnification!)

Originally, people didn't think tuberculosis was contagious; they thought some people were just destined to get sick. A number of famous writers, including English poets John Keats and Percy Bysshe Shelley, fell ill. That gave people the idea that tuberculosis affected only fancy rich people and that it made them more attractive, smarter, and more creative. Friends of the French author Victor Hugo joked that he'd have been a better writer if he'd gotten the disease. The British poet Lord Byron once said he wouldn't mind catching it.

I SHOULD LIKE TO DIE OF A CONSUMPTION, BECAUSE THE LADIES WOULD ALL SAY, "LOOK AT THAT POOR BYRON. HOW INTERESTING HE LOOKS IN DYING."

Weirdly, it became sort of stylish to get tuberculosis. Women who weren't sick started putting rice powder on their faces so they'd look as pale as those who were ill. Can you imagine wishing for an infection that would eat away at your lungs and leave you struggling to breathe? People eventually stopped thinking tuberculosis was so cool once they realized it was a contagious disease you could catch on the streets, not some fancy condition you inherited from your rich ancestors.

HEALTH CARE HEROES

Tuberculosis was a huge problem in New York City in the late 1800s, when a young nurse named Lillian Wald (1867–1940) was studying to be a doctor. She organized nursing classes for immigrants in the city's Lower East Side. One day, a little girl grabbed Wald and took her to see her mother, who was sick.

Lillian Wald

"*Over broken asphalt, over dirty mattresses and heaps of refuse we went. . . . There were two rooms and a family of seven not only lived here but shared their quarters with boarders. . . . {I felt} ashamed of being a part of society that permitted such conditions to exist. . . . What I had seen had shown me where my path lay.*"

—LILLIAN WALD

Wald suggested that she and another nurse move to that part of the city so they could live among the people they served. That way, people could get to know and trust their nurses. She became America's first public health nurse. Later, Wald suggested that nurses also be assigned to schools; she's the reason you probably have a nurse in your school today.

Robert Koch made it his mission to figure out what caused tuberculosis. Koch was already kind of a scientific hotshot by then. He'd discovered the bacterium that causes anthrax, a disease that mostly affects livestock. But like all scientists, Koch was standing on the shoulders of researchers who came before him, including people like Snow, who'd started to figure things out at the water pump. The truth is, scientists had been inching closer to an understanding of germs for hundreds of years.

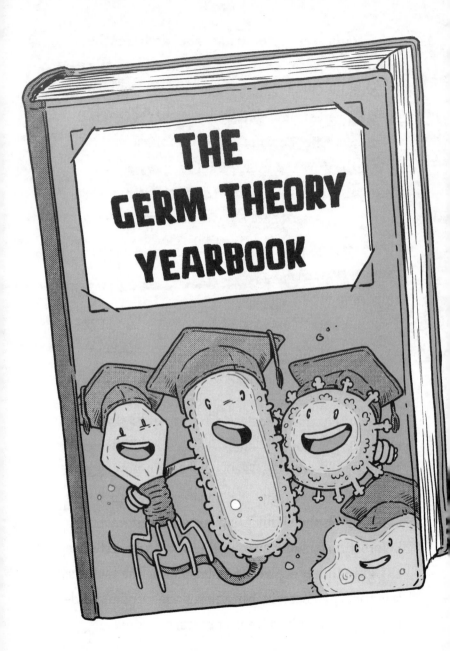

MOST LIKELY TO HANG OUT WITH POND SCUM

A Dutch father-son team, Hans and Zacharias Janssen, built the first compound microscope in 1590, but it was Antoni van Leeuwenhoek (1632–1723) who really made microscopes useful for the study of disease in the 1600s. He made simple microscopes with much greater magnification and was the first to observe single-celled organisms, in water samples from a pond.

MOST LIKELY TO DISPROVE A BELOVED IDEA AND BE IGNORED (ALSO BEST-WIG AWARD)

Back in Francesco Redi's time (1626-1697), there was a popular (but wrong) theory called spontaneous generation, the idea that living things like maggots, which we now know hatch from flies' eggs, could somehow just arise from nonliving matter. Redi designed an experiment to find out if that was true. He put some meat in containers, covered half of them, and left the other half open. If the maggots were arising from the meat, they should have appeared on all the samples, but they showed up only on the ones that were open to the air, where flies could lay their eggs. This was important in the development of germ theory because it helped prove that living things— including disease-causing microbes—did not magically appear from nonliving matter.

MOST LIKELY TO DISPROVE A BELOVED IDEA AND BE IGNORED BECAUSE OF HER GENDER

Maria Sibylla Merian (1647-1717) also helped disprove the theory of spontaneous generation. She was doing her work around the same time as Redi, but as a young woman, she didn't get the same attention or credit. People looked at her as more artist than scientist.

But Merian was also an entomologist, someone who studies insects. She was among the first to document the life cycle of caterpillars and butterflies, showing that caterpillars hatch from eggs instead of simply rising from the mud, as many people imagined back then.

MOST LIKELY TO NAG YOU TO WASH YOUR HANDS

In 1846, a Hungarian doctor named Ignaz Semmelweis (1818–1865) began working at a maternity hospital and noticed that women were dying of infection much more often when their babies were delivered in one division, where doctors worked, than in the other, where women were cared for by midwives (women who help with childbirth but aren't doctors). Semmelweis realized the doctors were conducting autopsies on people who'd died of infection and then delivering babies without washing their hands. Gross, right? Semmelweis thought so, too.

The following year, he made a rule that doctors had to wash their hands with a chlorine solution before delivering babies. Right away the death rates dropped. Semmelweis might not have understood germs yet, but he proved that handwashing was a good way to get rid of them.

MOST LIKELY TO SUCCEED (AT GETTING PEOPLE TO UNDERSTAND GERMS)

French scientist Louis Pasteur, who lived from 1822 to 1895, was finally able to confirm the germ theory, not by studying diseases at first but by studying drinks. Pasteur proved that microbes are the reason drinks like wine and milk go sour after a while. In 1862, he

came up with a process to kill bacteria in liq-uids by boiling and cooling. This process, now called pasteurization, is still used today. Pas-teur also did experiments to show that Redi was right about spontaneous generation not being a thing; bacteria had to be introduced from somewhere. Pasteur went on to use the ideas of germ theory to study chicken chol-era, anthrax, tuberculosis, and smallpox. Pasteur came up with a new way to vaccinate people, using microbes that were attenuated, or deactivated, so they'd no longer be able to make people so sick.

Louis Pasteur and Robert Koch were studying bacteria at the same time, so you might think they'd end up being pals.

Nope. They were fierce rivals. But both made huge contributions to our understanding of diseases caused by bacteria. Koch identified *Mycobacterium tuberculosis,* the bacterium that causes tuberculosis. Pasteur's work led to the development of a vaccine that was first given to people in 1921. It wasn't all that effective, though, so outbreaks of the disease continued. And there was still no real cure.

But some people decided that fresh country air might prevent the disease and help those already suffering from it. A German doctor named Hermann Brehmer suggested that tuberculosis patients take "the cure" by spending time outside, eating healthy, and resting. It may not have been a real cure, but it wasn't bad advice. By 1922, there were hundreds of outdoorsy rest and treatment facilities, called sanatoriums, in the United States.

Tuberculosis patients at sanatoriums and "cure cottages," like this one in Saranac Lake, New York (1893), were encouraged to spend as much time outside as possible, even in cold weather.

The real cure for tuberculosis would come with the discovery of antibiotics, drugs that kill bacteria.

In 1928, Alexander Fleming discovered penicillin, which was used in medicine beginning in 1941. It wasn't good for treating tuberculosis, but it led to research on other antibiotics, such as streptomycin, that would be effective. Finally, the world had a cure for tuberculosis!

You might be thinking that was the end of the disease, or maybe by now you've figured out that microbes are sneaky. Tuberculosis rates in the United States dropped more than 75 percent between 1953 and 1985, but since then the disease has made a comeback among people who have problems with their immune systems.

Globally, the World Health Organization estimates that tuberculosis made 10 million people sick in 2018 and killed 1.5 million that year.

ANTIBIOTIC BUSTERS

One reason tuberculosis continues to be such a threat is because some bacteria have become resistant to antibiotics. That means the drugs aren't able to kill the bacteria anymore.

When an infection is treated with antibiotics, most bacteria are killed, except for the few that are most resistant.

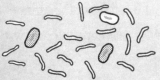

Those bacteria survive . . .

. . . and reproduce by splitting themselves, creating even more bacteria that are resistant.

Since the nonresistant bacteria die when treated with antibiotics, they can't pass on their traits. That includes the trait of being susceptible to antibiotics, so a bigger and bigger portion of the bacterial population becomes resistant.

The overuse of antibiotics has made the problem of resistance even worse. In 2016, the CDC estimated that 30 percent of antibiotics American doctors were prescribing weren't actually needed. The more antibiotics people take, the more bacteria become resistant, so the CDC is working to decrease the use of antibiotics in the United States, and doctors are being more careful to prescribe these drugs only when patients really need them.

Chances are, you'll need antibiotics for an illness or infection at some point. When you do, there are steps you can take to help prevent antibiotic resistance.

 BE A RESISTANCE FIGHTER!

1. Never take antibiotics unless your doctor prescribes them.

2. Always follow the directions your doctor gives you.

3. Don't stop taking antibiotics early, even if you start to feel better.

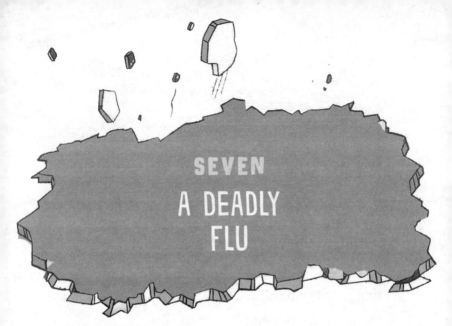

SEVEN
A DEADLY FLU

Maybe you've been reading this book and thinking, "Wow . . . all those diseases from history sure were something!" But this is the chapter where things start to get real, because the microbes that cause influenza are still wreaking havoc all over the world. You've probably had a flu shot to protect you from getting this disease, and because that vaccine isn't 100 percent effective, there's a good chance you've also had the flu. If you have, you'll remember the symptoms that make flu patients feel so crummy.

SORE THROAT   DRY COUGH   WEAKNESS AND
FATIGUE

CHILLS   FEVER

HEADACHE   LOSS OF
APPETITE

Most people who get the flu feel sick for a week or two and then get better, but a small percentage of people experience more serious illness. The World Health Organization estimates that about a billion people get the flu each year, and as many as 650,000 of them die. In developed nations, most of those who die are elderly or have other health problems. But some flu outbreaks have been much more deadly.

Influenza has been around for thousands of years, going all the way back to ancient Greece. The first influenza pandemic (at least, the first one that all experts agree on) started in 1580, when the disease spread from Asia through Africa and Europe and possibly to the Americas as well. There were two flu pandemics in the eighteenth century and another two in the nineteenth century. But the outbreak that really made history happened in 1918.

WORLD WAR I WAS RAGING THEN, WITH SOLDIERS TRAVELING ALL OVER THE GLOBE.

FRANCE

SPAIN

ONE MORNING IN MARCH, A MESS HALL COOK NAMED ALBERT GITCHELL SHOWED UP AT THE INFIRMARY AT CAMP FUNSTON IN KANSAS COMPLAINING OF A SORE THROAT, HEADACHE, AND FEVER.

BY LUNCHTIME, MORE THAN A HUNDRED OTHER MEN HAD JOINED HIM, ALL WITH SIMILAR SYMPTOMS.

KING ALFONSO XIII OF SPAIN GOT SICK IN MAY, ALONG WITH HIS PRIME MINISTER AND CABINET.

THE 1918 OUTBREAK HAD BECOME A PANDEMIC . . .

Influenza

. . . AND IT WAS ONLY GETTING STARTED.

Influenza cases quieted down a bit with the arrival of summer but roared back with a vengeance in August. The second wave was deadlier and hit young adults, who were usually less vulnerable to disease.

At the time, people didn't know if influenza was caused by a virus or bacteria, and there was no cure or vaccine. All public health officials could do was offer advice to try to stop the spread. They told people to avoid crowds, use a hankie when they sneezed, and wash their hands often. Many communities closed public schools, theaters, and places of worship. They banned mass gatherings and spitting in the street.

Some cities ordered quarantines or required people to wear masks in public to slow the spread of germs. Most people did a decent job following the rules, at least at first. America was still at war, so citizens were feeling patriotic and were willing to make sacrifices to contain the disease. There was public pressure to do the right thing; if you didn't, you were looked at as an unpatriotic slacker.

But it wasn't long before some people got tired of all those rules. The mayor of Oakland, California, was arrested for not wearing a mask in a Sacramento hotel lobby. Newspaper reports said he was furious about having to follow the rules like everybody else.

In some countries, especially those that were at war, news about the influenza pandemic was censored. The government kept it secret and prevented newspapers from reporting on it, because they didn't want to hurt morale. They needed people to keep supporting the war effort. One Italian newspaper was reporting the death tolls from the flu every day until the government ordered it to stop because people were panicking.

When people didn't get updates on the pandemic, they stopped worrying about it so much. They also stopped following the rules that had been put in place to keep them healthy. So the flu spread more quickly. When the newsboys became sick and stopped delivering papers, people heard even less about the outbreak. They went back to church and forgot to wear their masks, and the unreported death toll rose so quickly that hospitals and gravediggers had a hard time keeping up. It turned out that when a country pretended an outbreak wasn't happening, that didn't make the disease go away; it just made things a lot worse.

SOMEWHERE ELSE'S FLU

The 1918 influenza outbreak is commonly referred to as the Spanish flu. Hearing that, many people assume the first confirmed cases occurred in Spain, but you already know that's not true. The first outbreak was recorded in Kansas.

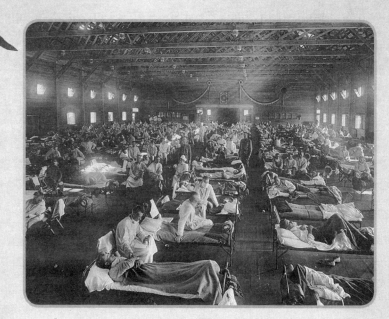

An emergency hospital at Camp Funston in Kansas during the influenza pandemic

So why isn't it called the Kansas flu? Part of the answer has to do with all that censorship happening in countries that were involved in World War I. Spain was neutral in the war, so newspapers there were allowed to do their job and tell the people of Spain what was happening. That made it *look* as if the virus had attacked Spain first, even though it was just as bad, if not worse, in countries that were trying to cover it up.

When the virus first began to spread, it was called different names all over the world.

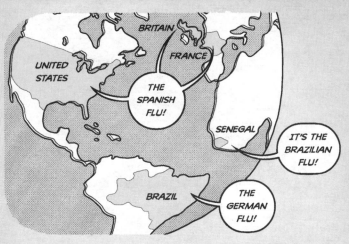

When it became clear that the outbreak was a real-deal pandemic, the world had to agree on a name for it. The United States and Britain were powerful nations back then, so even though the name they had chosen wasn't accurate, it stuck.

This blame-somebody-else strategy isn't just an influenza thing. When disease breaks out in a country, it's still common for government leaders to try to blame everything on another nation to take the focus off what they might or might not be doing to help their own people.

American cities handled the 1918 influenza outbreak in different ways. Philadelphia allowed public gatherings and even held a parade.

Held on September 28, 1918, the Liberty Loan parade was organized to promote government bonds, which raised money for the troops in World War I.

Within four months, twelve thousand people in Philadelphia had died of the flu. St. Louis, which shut down its schools, churches, and theaters and didn't allow public gatherings, had a much lower death rate. But at the end of World War I, St. Louis opened everything back up, and the city saw another wave of illness two weeks later.

The outbreak lasted into 1919 and claimed at least 50 million lives around the world. Some scientists say that number might be closer to 100 million; it's hard to know for sure because some hard-hit nations weren't keeping statistics.

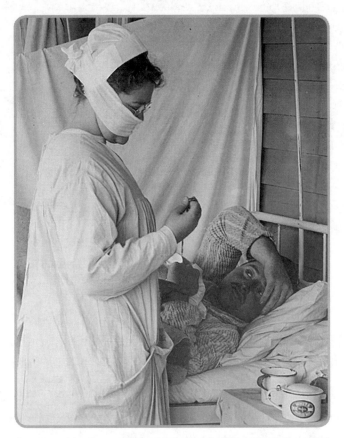

A nurse treats a patient at the Walter Reed Hospital flu ward during the pandemic.

HEALTH CARE HEROES

The illness that swept the globe in 1918 and 1919 was twenty-five times as deadly as typical influenza. Was it bacterial or viral? And why was it so lethal? Scientists would spend decades looking for answers.

In the 1920s and 1930s, researchers discovered that influenza affects not only people but also pigs—and that the disease could be transmitted from one species to another. In 1933, researchers in London did an experiment to see if ferrets would get the flu if they were inoculated with nasal washings from people who were sick. Those samples were filtered to get rid of any bacteria (which are bigger than viruses). The ferrets came down with pretty much all the same symptoms the people had.

And then—in what you might imagine was an act of revenge—one of those ferrets sneezed in a researcher's face, and he got sick, too! The scientists then found that samples from the sneezed-on researcher could be used to infect more ferrets. This led them to conclude that influenza was viral and not bacterial, and it paved the way for researchers Thomas Francis Jr. (1900–1969) and Jonas Salk (1914–1995) to develop a vaccine in the 1940s.

Thomas Francis Jr.   Jonas Salk

But scientists were still left wondering about that 1918 pandemic. What had made it so much deadlier than the usual flu? In 1951, a microbiologist named Johan Hultin went searching for answers in Alaska.

Hultin traveled to Brevig Mission, where influenza had devastated the Inuit people in 1918, sweeping through the village so quickly that some victims had to be buried in a mass grave. The researcher wondered if he might find influenza samples preserved in the permafrost, so he asked for permission to excavate, or dig up, that grave. His team was able to obtain lung tissue samples from several bodies they found at the site.

It wasn't easy getting the samples back to Hultin's lab in Iowa. They kept thawing, and Hultin had to keep refreezing them during his little plane's fuel stops. Back in the lab, Hultin tried to grow the virus by injecting the lung tissue into chicken eggs. His attempts didn't work—science is like that sometimes—so it looked as if his trip to Alaska had been for nothing. But that would change when Ann Reid and Jeffery Taubenberger came along.

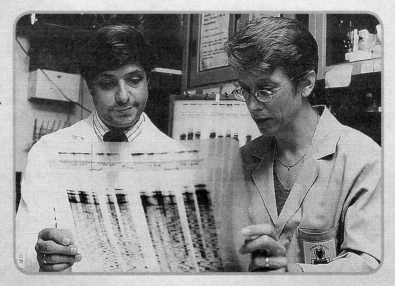

Scientists Jeffery Taubenberger and Ann Reid study a genetic sequence from the 1918 influenza virus.

In 1996, Taubenberger and Reid began studying influenza lung tissue from a soldier who'd died in a military camp in 1918. They used it to sequence fragments of the virus's RNA, or genetic material. Because the sample was old and had been damaged, they couldn't finish their work, but they wrote about it anyway in the journal *Science*.

Hultin read the article and reached out to tell its authors about the sample *he* had used to try to identify the flu virus. Hultin was in his seventies by then, but he offered to go back to Alaska to get another sample. Taubenberger and Reid took him up on that and used the new sample to complete their work.

The team of scientists finished sequencing the RNA and realized that it was similar to a virus they'd seen before—one that caused bird flu. They reconstructed the virus in the laboratory so more research could be done to learn about the 1918 pandemic and to prevent future outbreaks.

Influenza outbreaks remain a threat today; there's always the concern that a strain that usually affects birds or other animals could make the jump to infect people. That happened in 1997, when a three-year-old child in Hong Kong was admitted to the hospital with flu symptoms and later died. Scientists discovered that the child was infected with H5N1, a type of influenza that had only been seen in birds before.

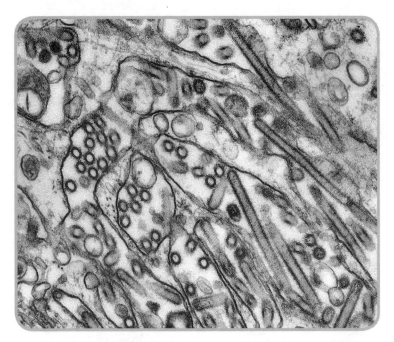

The rod and small circle shapes in this photo are H5N1 viruses, as seen with a scanning electron microscope.

The virus was traced to poultry markets in Hong Kong, and the government killed more than a million chickens to prevent its spread. Fortunately, the new flu strain hasn't spread widely. So far, people typically catch H5N1 only through close contact with infected chickens or other birds. Scientists have developed a vaccine for the new bird flu and are stockpiling it in case the virus mutates to spread more easily.

VACCINATION VARIATIONS

After reading about all this scientific progress and research, you might be wondering why people still get the flu every year. It's because there are multiple strains, or types, of flu out there, and researchers still haven't come up with a single vaccine that protects people against all of them. The virus mutates, or changes, and there's no way for researchers to know which strains will be most common in a given flu season. So the World Health Organization makes predictions, and those are the strains included in that season's vaccine.

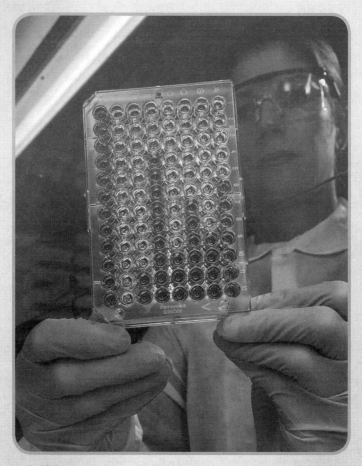

A CDC scientist runs tests to help determine which viruses to include in a seasonal flu vaccine in 2019.

A whole team of experts works on this process, but it's still a challenge. The team has to decide in February which strains of virus to include for vaccinations that will start in October. If a new strain of influenza surfaces after the deadline, it can't be included, so the vaccine is only partially effective. The same thing happens if the predictions aren't quite right. Scientists continue to work on a universal vaccine that would include all the strains and wouldn't need to be updated every year. But in the meantime, even flu vaccines that provide partial protection keep millions of people from getting sick and may result in milder symptoms for those who *do* become ill.

EIGHT

THE BATTLE AGAINST POLIO

If you know someone who was alive in the 1940s and 1950s, ask them what they remember about polio. Chances are, they'll tell you stories about not being allowed to swim in pools or lakes during the summer for fear they'd catch the dreaded disease. Maybe they remember celebrating when the news arrived that there was a successful vaccine.

Polio is an intestinal infection caused by a virus. Like cholera, it's transmitted when people eat or drink something that's contaminated with feces, or poop, that carries the virus. (That's why some cases were connected to swimming pools and lakes, and why your grandparents or great-grandparents might have been kept out of the water some summers when they were growing up.) Polio can also spread through droplets in the air when an infected person sneezes or coughs, or when someone touches something that's contaminated and then puts their hand in their mouth.

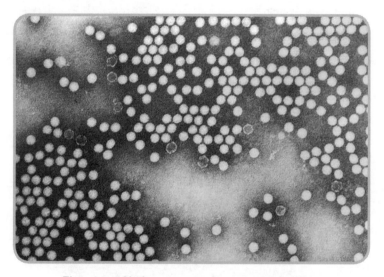

The virus that causes polio, as seen with a transmission electron microscope

Most people who catch polio are asymptomatic, which means they have no symptoms and don't even know they're infected. About one in four people gets a mild illness like the flu, with fever, headache, and sore throat. But in about one percent of polio cases, the virus causes severe illness that can lead to paralysis or death.

The first major polio outbreak in the United States happened in 1894 in Vermont. Eighteen people died, and dozens more were paralyzed, most of them children under the age of six. By the early 1900s, the disease was spreading through the country. It terrified parents, since most polio victims were children. There was a big push for research because the disease was shrouded in mystery. Why did it seem to be worst in the summer months? Why did it hit children so hard? And why did a small number of those who were infected become paralyzed?

HEALTH CARE HEROES

Karl Landsteiner (1868–1943) was an Austrian scientist who discovered that people have blood types. His work in the early 1900s led to the first successful blood transfusion.

In 1908, he turned his attention to polio and began searching for its cause. Could it be a virus? To find out, Landsteiner, working with another scientist, Erwin Popper, took some spinal cord fluid from a boy who had died of polio and put it through a filter to elimi-

Karl Landsteiner

nate any bacteria. Then he injected the filtered fluid into some animals to see if they would become infected. The fluid injection had no effect on guinea pigs, mice, or rabbits. But when Landsteiner tried it with monkeys, which are more similar to humans, the monkeys got sick with something that looked like polio. He had proved that the disease was likely caused by a virus, but a vaccine to prevent polio was still decades away.

In 1916, polio broke out in a Brooklyn, New York, neighborhood known as Pigtown, where a lot of Italian immigrants lived. Sick children were put in isolation wards. Swimming pools were closed, and people were afraid to let their kids go outside or even to open a window.

There was already a lot of discrimination against Italian Americans back then, so it's not surprising that when people were scared and pointing fingers about where the virus had come from, they blamed immigrants. Parts of Pigtown and other Italian neighborhoods were quarantined. The government even required certificates for children traveling out of New York City, proving they didn't have polio.

Six thousand people died in that outbreak, but it was after World War I that America really turned its attention to polio. Polio swept through the country every summer, and among the victims was future president Franklin Delano Roosevelt, who got sick in 1921, when he was thirty-nine years old.

"I first had a chill in the evening which lasted practically all night. The following morning the muscles of the right knee appeared weak and by afternoon I was unable to support my weight on my right leg. That evening the left knee began to weaken also and by the following morning I was unable to stand up."
—FRANKLIN DELANO ROOSEVELT

Political rivals tried to use Roosevelt's disability against him, saying he wasn't strong enough to be president. But he got elected anyway—four times! (That was before the United States had a limit of two terms for president.) Roosevelt tried not to be seen much in his

A rare photograph of Franklin Delano Roosevelt in his wheelchair

wheelchair while he was president. Instead of using it, he'd lean against a podium or a wall or take the arm of a friend for balance.

Roosevelt led the United States out of the Great Depression and through World War II, and he also led the way when it came to polio research. In 1934, he hosted a President's Birthday Ball fundraiser at a fancy New York City hotel on his birthday. There were hundreds of other balls, too, in cities and towns all over the country, where people waltzed and fox-trotted and raised over a million dollars. The Birthday Ball would become an annual event.

In 1938, Roosevelt founded an organization called the National Foundation for Infantile Paralysis (NFIP) to help polio patients and fund research. When a radio personality said everybody should send their pocket change to Roosevelt in a "march of dimes to reach all the way to the White House," people took that request seriously. They mailed the president *millions* of dimes!

Roosevelt's personal secretary Missy LeHand with some of the letters containing dimes that arrived at the White House in 1938

"The Government of the United States darned near stopped functioning because we couldn't clear away enough dimes."

—IRA T. SMITH, WHITE HOUSE MAIL ROOM

The NFIP renamed its fundraising branch the March of Dimes and assigned it to deal with the ongoing campaign (so poor Ira didn't have to keep counting all those dimes!). But polio wasn't defeated overnight. The summer outbreaks seemed to get worse every year, and there was still no vaccine or cure.

Early treatments for paralysis involved a lot of lying around. Doctors and nurses thought if patients moved their muscles the wrong way, deformities might result, so patients were stuck in bed with their bodies in casts and splints, unable to move for weeks or even months. They were held still so long that their muscles broke down—even muscles that polio hadn't affected.

HEALTH CARE HEROES

An Australian nurse named Elizabeth Kenny, who lived from 1880 to 1952, had different ideas for how to help polio patients. Instead of forcing them to rest, Kenny put hot packs on their damaged limbs and helped them carefully exercise their muscles. At first, doctors rejected Kenny's ideas, but it became hard for them to ignore how much her treatments were helping people. By the mid-1940s, the Kenny Method was the standard way American doctors and nurses treated polio patients.

Elizabeth Kenny

AN EQUAL-OPPORTUNITY DISEASE . . . WITH UNEQUAL TREATMENT

Diseases like cholera and tuberculosis had hit poor people hardest, but polio hit everyone.

The *Ladies' Home Journal* seemed bewildered that there was no way to buy safety.

"Once the terror stalks, mere wealth cannot buy immunity. The well-fed babies of the boulevards are no safer than gamins from the gutter."
—LADIES' HOME JOURNAL

Wealth couldn't buy immunity, but if you were fairly well off and white, you received better care. Polio outbreaks in America happened before the civil rights movement, so when Roosevelt created the Warm Springs treatment center in Georgia, the center treated only white people. His wife, Eleanor, suggested that the hospital build a cabin for African American polio victims, but her idea was rejected. Later, the NFIP donated money to the Tuskegee Institute to build a polio hospital for Black people.

The number of polio cases in the country continued to rise, and hit a peak in 1952. All the while, scientists worked to develop a vaccine.

ATTEMPTS TO DEVELOP A VACCINE IN THE 1930S DIDN'T WORK.

NOT ENOUGH WAS KNOWN ABOUT THE DISEASE, AND TESTS DONE ON EARLY VACCINES WERE CONDUCTED SO POORLY THAT THE DATA WAS WORTHLESS.

A RESEARCHER NAMED JOHN KOLMER TESTED A VACCINE HE'D DEVELOPED ON HIS FAMILY . . . AND EVENTUALLY ON MORE THAN TEN THOUSAND KIDS.

BUT HIS VACCINE CAUSED AT LEAST A DOZEN POLIO CASES AND AT LEAST SIX DEATHS. THE TROUBLING NEWS WAS ANNOUNCED AT AN AMERICAN PUBLIC HEALTH ASSOCIATION MEETING.

GENTLEMEN, THIS IS ONE TIME I WISH THE FLOOR WOULD OPEN UP AND SWALLOW ME.

But Salk's vaccine wasn't 100 percent effective. And there was a huge problem with the vaccine that came from one manufacturer called Cutter Laboratories. Some kids who'd received vaccines produced there got sick right after they were vaccinated and suffered paralysis in the arm where they'd been given the shot. Five children died. The Cutter vaccine was recalled, and the lab admitted there had been trouble with live virus remaining in its vaccine. That was a huge setback because even though the other suppliers' vaccines were safe, people were scared. For a while, fewer got vaccinated, and that led to big outbreaks of polio in Chicago and Boston.

After that problem with Salk's vaccine, Sabin started to get more attention. He'd kept working on his vaccine, which was administered orally (sometimes on sugar cubes), and eventually it replaced Salk's as the primary polio vaccine in the United States. It was cheaper and easier to give. After all,

The polio vaccine was often administered to children on sugar cubes.

what kid doesn't like a sugar cube better than a shot?

In 1955, a headline in the *New York Herald Tribune* shouted out, "Polio Victory May Spell End of All Virus Diseases." Polio had all but been eliminated in the United States and was declining around the globe. Could the world eradicate polio? The WHO launched a major vaccination effort with a goal of getting rid of polio by 2005, but that deadline came and went. Many people who are infected with polio don't have symptoms, so truly getting rid of the virus would mean vaccinating pretty much everyone on the planet. Civil wars and other conflicts make parts of the world too dangerous for health care workers, so that goal has yet to be achieved.

NINE

THE NEW GERMS IN TOWN

There used to be a lot of talk about getting rid of infectious diseases entirely; one day, they'd be nothing more than a line in a textbook or an exhibit in a museum. But the people who made those hopeful predictions were thinking about diseases they knew—the ones that had been around for a long time. They didn't realize how quickly microbes can change, evolve, and reproduce. And they weren't counting on new germs showing up.

The world has more people now. They live in crowded places and travel more than they used to. Many fly around the world on airplanes. Others are forced to leave their homes because of war, famine, or persecution. And wherever people go, microbes go, too. Since 1970, the world has seen the emergence of more than forty new diseases—illnesses never before seen in humans.

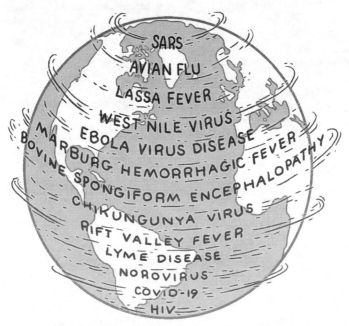

One problem with emerging diseases is that no one recognizes them when they first show up. That was the case with HIV, which attacks the body's immune system and can lead to AIDS. Scientists now believe this virus may have been infecting people as far back as the late 1800s. They think it may have jumped from chimpanzees to humans, perhaps when a hunter was infected. From there, it spread quietly around the world until 1981, when doctors in several American cities noticed unusual infections and illnesses showing up in previously healthy men. Those patients were infected with the virus we now know as HIV.

HIV = human immunodeficiency virus, an infection that attacks the body's immune system

AIDS—acquired immunodeficiency syndrome, a term that applies to the most advanced stages of HIV infection, when a person may develop serious illnesses that take advantage of a weakened immune system

People with AIDS often lose weight very quickly and are exhausted all the time. Other symptoms of HIV infection can include fever, night sweats, and swollen lymph glands. Because HIV affects a person's immune system, it makes them vulnerable to other dangerous microbes as well.

The Centers for Disease Control and Prevention, a US government agency that deals with public health issues, began to investigate the outbreak, but prejudice slowed research on HIV/AIDS. The first people to get sick with it in the United States were gay men, who faced a lot of discrimination and bigotry. Some government leaders didn't support funding research for an illness that seemed to affect only people who were gay.

You might be thinking that those government leaders didn't have much empathy, or concern for others, and that's true. They were also wrong about who could be affected by HIV.

This virus only spreads through certain bodily fluids. It can be transmitted during sexual contact and also through blood. That meant people who used drugs and shared needles to inject them could be infected with the virus, and so could anyone who had to get a blood transfusion because they were sick or needed surgery. (When people donate blood now, it's screened for the virus, but that system wasn't in place during the initial outbreak in the United States.) One big problem with HIV is that people can be infected for a long time before they develop symptoms, which means they can transmit the virus to others without knowing they have it.

In early 1983, researchers at the Pasteur Institute in Paris discovered that HIV was a new human virus. The following year, American researcher Robert Gallo published similar research and determined that HIV was the cause of AIDS.

Françoise Barré-Sinoussi

Luc Montagnier

Harald zur Hausen

Robert Gallo

The work of these researchers led to the development of a blood test for HIV.

Ronald Reagan was president of the United States when the HIV/AIDS epidemic began, but it was years before he gave a speech about it. All that time, one of his own friends was fighting the disease.

Actor Rock Hudson (left) with Nancy Reagan and President Ronald Reagan at a White House dinner in 1984

Rock Hudson was a famous movie star who had been diagnosed with AIDS but kept it a secret for a long time because of the stigma that went along with the illness. He made headlines in 1985 as the first celebrity to die of AIDS-related illnesses. Hudson wasn't just any movie star; he was a handsome Hollywood hero, so his death forced many people to reevaluate their biases about AIDS. That included the president. Two years after his friend's death, Reagan gave a speech about the epidemic. By then, the disease had spread to all fifty states and killed twenty thousand people. Protesters thought it was too little, and way too late.

Activists pushed for more research funding. One of them was Larry Kramer, who founded ACT UP, the AIDS Coalition to Unleash Power. The group staged demonstrations and criticized government officials for failing to do more about AIDS.

Larry Kramer

Eventually, an increase in research funding led to a treatment and prevention drug for AIDS. That first medicine, called azidothymidine, or AZT, doesn't cure AIDS, but it helps patients live longer lives. Researchers are still working on a vaccine to prevent HIV infection, but the development of AZT and, later, other HIV drugs was a huge breakthrough—one that turned HIV infection into a diagnosis that people live with instead of one that kills them. Today, many people who are HIV positive take a combination of those drugs and are able to live long, healthy lives.

HEALTH CARE HEROES

In 2003, microbiologist Karidia Diallo helped launch an effort called the US President's Emergency Plan for AIDS Relief. Its goal was to bring treatment to and save lives in sub-Saharan Africa, where AIDS was a huge problem. But it was impossible to do that work without modern laboratories and people trained to work in them. So Diallo and her colleagues came up with new ways to diagnose patients, trained health care workers, and improved labs throughout the continent.

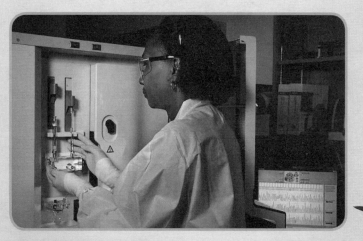

CDC scientist Karidia Diallo prepares to analyze samples to be used in drug-resistance testing, 2007.

Scientists are still working on HIV/AIDS research, even as they battle other emerging microbes. Diseases caused by filoviruses (named for their filament-like, or thready, structure) have jumped from animals to people and made headlines around the world. Ebola is the most famous—and the most feared of them all.

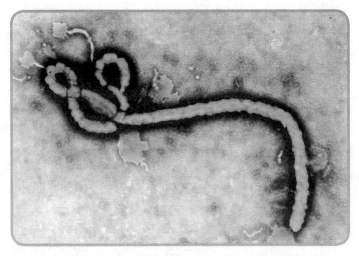

Ebola virus, as seen with a transmission electron microscope at the CDC

Ebola virus disease starts out like the flu. Patients may have a fever, muscle pains, a sore throat, and fatigue. But the disease takes a horrific turn when it progresses to what's called its wet phase, with vomiting, diarrhea, and often bleeding from the mouth, nose, and skin. More than half of all Ebola virus cases are fatal, with most patients dying about a week after symptoms begin.

Because the symptoms are so dramatic, health care workers tend to notice right away when an Ebola virus outbreak begins, so patients can be isolated to prevent the spread. That's one reason Ebola hasn't become a pandemic. The other good news about Ebola is that it doesn't spread easily from person to person. It's transmitted only through close contact with an infected person's blood or other body fluids, and people who are infected typically show symptoms within a week or two.

Ebola can infect apes, monkeys, and humans, but its original host—the place it started in nature—is likely a kind of fruit-eating bat that lives in Africa. When people come in close contact with those bats, the virus can jump species and infect humans. That first happened in 1976 in the Democratic Republic of the Congo (DRC), which was then called Zaire.

Since then, the virus has killed tens of thousands of people in Africa. There's still no cure for Ebola virus disease, but a vaccine to prevent it was approved in 2019. It's called Ervebo and is now being used to try to contain outbreaks.

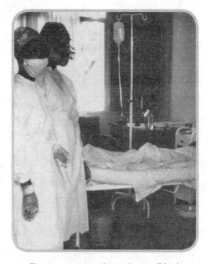

Two nurses treat an Ebola patient during the 1976 outbreak.

HEALTH CARE HEROES

It took a whole bunch of researchers to lay the groundwork for that Ebola vaccine, starting with the person who first discovered the virus. Belgian researcher Peter Piot wrote a book about his work and often gets much of the credit for the discovery. But that story needs a little smashing.

DISCOVERER OF EBOLA

Dr. Piot worked at the Institute of Tropical Medicine in Antwerp, Belgium. He was part of the team that first isolated Ebola from a patient's blood sample and saw the lasso-shaped virus with an electron microscope. But Piot and the other team members didn't know what it was. It looked sort of like Marburg, another deadly filovirus, but maybe it was something new. Either way, the lab wasn't equipped to work with a virus as dangerous as Marburg, so they sent the sample to two other labs that were. One was at the CDC in Atlanta, where Dr. Patricia Webb and her colleagues ran tests and determined that the virus wasn't Marburg. It was something new.

Webb often gets left out of the Ebola discovery story. And so does the Congolese epidemiologist who had sent that sample to the lab where Piot worked.

Dr. Jean-Jacques Muyembe was called to investigate the very first Ebola outbreak in 1976, when nobody knew what was making people so sick. Muyembe was examining patients without gloves or protective equipment—it's a

Dr. Jean–Jacques Muyembe

wonder he didn't get infected—and noticed symptoms he'd never seen before. Could it be a brand-new disease? Muyembe took blood samples from a local nun who was infected and sent them to that lab in Belgium, where he knew the researchers had an electron microscope for viewing the virus. Muyembe is mentioned in Piot's book, but he rarely gets credit for his role in the discovery of Ebola. Without Muyembe's observations on the ground in central Africa, Piot and the other scientists couldn't have done their work.

Muyembe was the first virologist ever to see an Ebola patient, and since his discovery, he's continued to fight the disease in the Democratic Republic of the Congo. In 2020, he was seventy-eight years old and dealing with an ongoing Ebola outbreak when he was tasked with handling his country's response to a totally different epidemic. Another new disease had emerged—one that would circle the globe in a matter of weeks, affecting nearly every nation. It was called COVID-19.

A CDC illustration of the virus that causes COVID-19

On the last day of 2019, health officials in China reported an unusual cluster of pneumonia cases in the city of Wuhan. A week later, researchers had identified the cause of this illness. It was a brand-new coronavirus, now called SARS-CoV-2. The disease it causes was named COVID-19, short for "coronavirus disease 2019."

While SARS-CoV-2 was new, other coronaviruses have been around for a long time. "Coronavirus" comes from the Latin word for "crown"—the viruses have a spiky, crownlike structure. Not all coronaviruses are dangerous; some cause the common cold.

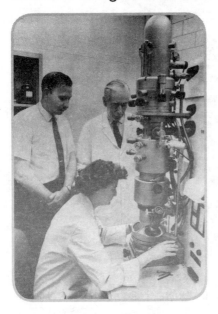

Researcher June Almeida (seated) identified the first coronavirus known to cause disease in humans in 1966, while she was part of a team studying the common cold.

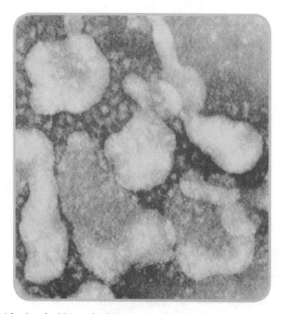

Almeida took this photograph of a coronavirus, as seen with an electron microscope in 1966.

But even before the COVID-19 pandemic, scientists knew that this type of virus could be deadly. A coronavirus that causes a disease called SARS (severe acute respiratory syndrome) was responsible for the first pandemic of the twenty-first century, killing 774 people during an outbreak from 2002 to 2003. It didn't last long, because SARS wasn't super easy to transmit from one person to another. The only exception was a small group of people scientists called super-spreaders.

Super-Spreader might sound like a comic-book hero, but it's actually a person who is highly contagious and spreads an illness to an unusually large number of people. Scientists aren't sure why. Maybe it's because they're infected but don't feel sick enough to stay home, or perhaps they give off more virus particles than is typical. There were a handful of super-spreaders of SARS who infected large numbers of people. One of them was a doctor who had been sick but started feeling a little better, so he decided to travel from mainland China to Hong Kong for a wedding. The man, who got sicker after he arrived, infected at least sixteen people in the hotel where he stayed.

SUPER-SPREADER TYPHOID MARY

A magazine illustration of Typhoid Mary from 1909

Super-spreaders can transmit all kinds of diseases. The most famous super-spreader in history was a woman named Mary Mallon, also known as Typhoid Mary. She worked as a cook in the early 1900s and was a carrier of the bacterium that causes typhoid fever. She never got sick herself, but she passed the microbe on to dozens of other people who did. When health officials figured out what was happening, they put her into quarantine to keep her from spreading the disease anymore.

The coronavirus that causes SARS was the first of its kind to result in serious illness in humans, but it wouldn't be the last. MERS, or Middle East respiratory syndrome, a disease with similar symptoms, showed up in Saudi Arabia in 2012. It was even deadlier than SARS, but fortunately it doesn't spread easily between people, so there's never been a big outbreak.

And then came COVID-19, another coronavirus disease with similar symptoms and one big difference—it's much more contagious, spreading easily through the air when people are in the same space, coughing, sneezing, singing, or even just talking. This new disease took off in a way that SARS and MERS hadn't. After the first cases were reported in China in

December 2019, the virus raced around the world until it had reached nearly every corner of the globe.

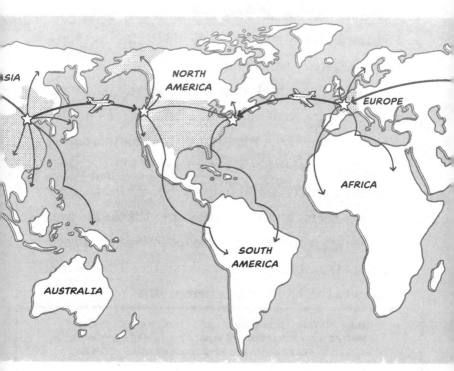

The first known case in the United States was reported in Washington State, when a man who'd recently returned from China got sick. Within a week, the National Institutes of Health (NIH) announced it was starting research to try to develop a vaccine. But vaccines take time to develop—usually years—and the virus traveled fast.

On January 31, 2020, the US government restricted travel from China. But it was already too late: the number of cases continued to grow in February, and on March 11, the World Health Organization declared a pandemic.

You might think that world leaders would have learned a lot from all the disease outbreaks in history, so they'd be pretty well prepared for this one. It was 2020, right? Shouldn't scientists know how to handle a pandemic? The truth is, scientists had some good ideas for how to slow the spread of the disease. But some government officials took their advice better than others, and leaders around the world handled the outbreak in different ways.

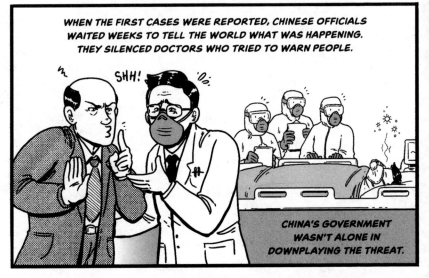

WHEN THE FIRST CASES WERE REPORTED, CHINESE OFFICIALS WAITED WEEKS TO TELL THE WORLD WHAT WAS HAPPENING. THEY SILENCED DOCTORS WHO TRIED TO WARN PEOPLE.

SHH!

CHINA'S GOVERNMENT WASN'T ALONE IN DOWNPLAYING THE THREAT.

BRAZIL'S PRESIDENT, JAIR BOLSONARO, WOULDN'T WEAR ONE, EITHER. A JUDGE FINALLY ORDERED HIM TO PUT ONE ON WHEN HE WAS OUT IN PUBLIC OR FACE A FINE.

IT WON'T BE A LITTLE COLD THAT WILL KNOCK ME DOWN.

BOLSONARO CONTRACTED COVID-19 IN JULY.

THE BRITISH PRIME MINISTER, BORIS JOHNSON, DIDN'T FOLLOW HEALTH EXPERTS' ADVICE, EITHER.

"I was at a hospital the other night. . . . There were actually a few coronavirus patients, and I shook hands with everybody."

THAT WAS IN EARLY MARCH. AT THE END OF THE MONTH, JOHNSON TESTED POSITIVE FOR COVID-19 AND SPENT A WEEK IN THE HOSPITAL.

LEADERS OF ITALY AND SOUTH KOREA ALSO PLAYED DOWN THE PANDEMIC AT FIRST. BUT THEY GOT SERIOUS AND TURNED THINGS AROUND AFTER MAJOR OUTBREAKS IN THEIR COUNTRIES.

GIUSEPPE CONTE
ITALY

MOON JAE-IN
SOUTH KOREA

PRIME MINISTER ANGELA MERKEL OF GERMANY WAS A SCIENTIST BEFORE SHE STARTED RUNNING A COUNTRY. SHE TOOK A DIFFERENT APPROACH...

... TELLING HER CITIZENS RIGHT AWAY THAT THE DISEASE WAS SERIOUS. SHE EXPLAINED HOW IT SPREAD AND IMPLEMENTED SOCIAL DISTANCING AND MASS TESTING.

NEW ZEALAND PRIME MINISTER JACINDA ARDERN TOOK A SIMILAR APPROACH, LAUNCHING MASSIVE TESTING AND LOCKDOWNS WHEN THE NATION HAD ONLY ABOUT ONE HUNDRED CASES.

WE MUST GO HARD, AND GO EARLY. WE MUST DO EVERYTHING WE CAN TO PROTECT NEW ZEALANDERS' HEALTH.

MARCH 14, 2020

BY MIDSUMMER, AS OTHER NATIONS CONTINUED TO BATTLE MAJOR OUTBREAKS, NEW ZEALAND HAD JUST A HANDFUL OF ACTIVE CASES, AND FEWER THAN TWO DOZEN DEATHS.

World leaders who said COVID-19 was no big deal were wrong. Schools closed around the world, and kids found themselves learning in front of computer screens instead of in the classroom. Professional sports were canceled. Even the summer Olympic Games were affected. It was only the fourth time in the history of the Olympics that the games were canceled. The other cancellations were during World War I and World War II.

By the end of September 2020, COVID-19 had killed more than a million people around the world. Millions more had lost their jobs when businesses were temporarily closed. The economic downturn prompted some governments to lift stay-at-home orders while the disease was still spreading, and then infection rates started climbing again. All the while, people held out hope that scientists would develop a safe and effective vaccine.

AN EPIDEMIC OF RACISM

Remember how Jewish people were blamed and persecuted during the Black Death in medieval times? The same thing happened to Eastern European immigrants in New York

City when cholera and a disease called typhus broke out there in the late 1800s. And in the spring of 1900, Chinese Americans were targeted after bubonic plague broke out in San Francisco.

You might think those days are long gone, but unfortunately, even in modern times, when disease outbreaks happen, open displays of hate and bigotry often increase, too. This happened to gay people during the HIV/AIDS epidemic. It happened to Navajo people in 1993, when an outbreak of a disease caused by hantavirus broke out in the Southwest, and reporters first called it "the Navajo disease," leading to fear and discrimination against Native people in the region.

During the SARS and COVID-19 outbreaks, racists targeted Asians and Asian Americans. The World Health Organization had changed its policy and stopped naming diseases after the places where they were first recorded in an attempt to avoid that sort of prejudice. But some US politicians insisted on calling COVID-19 made-up names based on the place it was first identified, which led to more prejudice. Asian American businesses were vandalized, and people were harassed on the streets or even physically assaulted.

This is an example of xenophobia, a fear of and hatred toward people from other countries, or strangers. If you observe it happening, you can help by speaking up. Sometimes it's good to think about how you might respond before you're actually in a situation where someone says something racist.

I'M A PERSON WHO WILL SPEAK UP AGAINST BIGOTRY.

Some ideas for what to say:

I DON'T FIND THAT FUNNY.

I'M SURPRISED TO HEAR YOU SAY THAT.

WHAT YOU'RE SAYING CAN REALLY HURT PEOPLE.

The COVID-19 pandemic continued to rage out of control through fall and winter. By May 2021, more than 150 million people around the world had been infected, and more than three million of them had died. The United States had recorded over half a million deaths—more than any other nation.

But there was also some hopeful news. After months of work, scientists developed vaccines that were safe and effective at preventing infection. In December 2020, the US Food and Drug Administration (FDA) issued Emergency Use Authorizations for the first two vaccines. Both had been tested on tens of thousands of volunteers and proved to be safe. Those studies also showed that the vaccines were about 95 percent effective.

Dr. Anthony Fauci, director of the National Institute of Allergy and Infectious Diseases, receives the COVID-19 vaccine in December 2020.

Vaccinations began immediately, starting with health care workers, senior citizens, and others who were most at risk. In February 2021, the United States gave Emergency Use Authorization for a third vaccine to fight COVID-19. Finally, the world seemed to be making progress against this deadly disease.

HEALTH CARE HEROES

Anthony Fauci is the director of the National Institute of Allergy and Infectious Diseases (NIAID) at the NIH.

Anthony Fauci

He's advised seven different US presidents on outbreaks of infectious diseases, including influenza, HIV/AIDS, Ebola, and COVID-19.

The first vaccines for COVID-19 were developed in less than a year, much faster than any other vaccine in history. But researchers didn't cut corners in developing or testing them. This timeline was possible because scientists had a head start.

Kizzmekia Corbett

Barney Graham

Kizzmekia Corbett, Barney Graham, and other researchers at NIH had been studying other coronaviruses for years before anyone had even heard of COVID-19. They had paid special attention to the spike proteins on the surface of a coronavirus, which are important in how the vaccines work. When the new virus emerged, the work that Corbett and Graham had already done paved the way for the speedy development of one of the first safe, effective vaccines for COVID-19.

Like other vaccines, those for COVID-19 work by tricking a person's body into producing antibodies for the virus. Some vaccines include a weakened (live) or inactivated (killed) version of a virus, but the first two vaccines approved to fight COVID-19 work differently. They use messenger RNA, or mRNA, a code that gives instructions for a person's cells to make a harmless piece of the spike protein found on the surface of the coronavirus. Once the cells produce that protein, the immune system kicks in and makes antibodies, just as it would if the person were actually infected with the virus.

TEN
PREVENTING THE NEXT PANDEMIC

So what does the future look like as far as public health? Scientists understand now that the next pandemic could be caused by a microbe no one has seen before. Changes happening around the globe have made outbreaks more likely. When people build dams, canals, and irrigation systems to supply water for growing food, they also create wet breeding sites for mosquitoes. When people cut down forests to make space for cities and farms, humans come into contact with wildlife that can carry disease. And when people crowd together in those new cities, unsanitary conditions can help diseases spread, too.

Experts believe that climate change, including global warming, is having a major effect on how infectious diseases emerge and spread. Many factors affect global climate, but scientists know that human action is responsible for much of the change we've seen over the past fifty to one hundred years. That's because certain gases, called greenhouse gases, block heat from escaping from the earth's atmosphere. Carbon dioxide is a greenhouse gas that is produced by human activities—everything from burning coal to run factories to burning fuel to drive cars. Oceans absorb most of the extra heat trapped by greenhouse gases. Rising sea temperatures can lead to more severe weather events, such as hurricanes and monsoons.

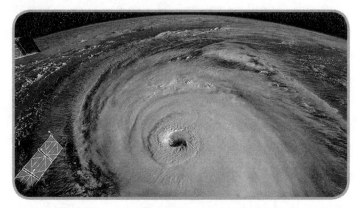

A view of Hurricane Florence from the International Space Station, 2018

What does this have to do with diseases? Climate can have a big impact on microbes that are spread by insects. Traditionally, diseases like malaria and yellow fever have been limited to the tropics, but scientists say that if climate change continues, the insects that spread those microbes are likely to creep north every year. One study found that by 2100, a billion people may be newly exposed to diseases carried by mosquitoes.

The Asian tiger mosquito (*Aedes albopictus*) can carry several viruses that cause disease in humans. Scientists predict it could spread to major cities like Chicago and Shanghai by 2050.

Climate change is also melting ice and permafrost soil that have been frozen for thousands of years. Scientists worry that ancient microbes—germs that no one alive has ever seen—could be released in the process.

WHAT CAN KIDS DO ABOUT CLIMATE CHANGE?

Sometimes with a problem as big as climate change, you may feel like there's nothing you can do about it. But everyone—including kids—can take a few small steps to make a difference.

When possible, walk or ride a bike instead of going places in the car.

Turn off electronics like TVs and computers when you're not using them.

Instead of throwing things away, reuse or recycle them whenever possible.

Carry a reusable water bottle so you can avoid single-use plastic bottles.

Try to take short showers, and turn off the sink water while you're brushing your teeth.

Climate change can also affect diseases that spread via contaminated water. Global warming has led to more severe droughts, so fewer people have access to clean water for drinking and washing their hands. Warmer ocean temperatures can lead to an increase in major storms, which cause flooding that can result in untreated sewage pouring into waterways. And when people's water sources are contaminated, they're vulnerable to all kinds of diseases that cause diarrhea, including cholera. Those same storms and floods sometimes force people from their homes, so many end up in refugee camps with poor sanitation.

That's the not-so-great news about the future of infectious diseases. The better news is that advances in science and technology have given us new ways to fight dangerous microbes. Vaccines have come a long way since the days when people were sniffing scab dust and scratching cowpox pus into their arms to prevent smallpox.

Today's vaccines go through a long, extensive series of tests to make sure they're safe before they're used to protect people from diseases. Vaccines aren't perfect. Some have side effects that can range from a sore arm or fever to more serious complications in a very small percentage of people. And they're not 100 percent effective, but some come close, and even those like the flu vaccine, which varies from year to year because the virus changes so quickly, save millions of lives.

But even today, not everyone makes decisions based on science. Remember those people who said Jenner's smallpox vaccine would make patients grow horns like cows? That myth got smashed a long time ago, but misinformation about vaccines still keeps some people from being protected from disease. One of those myths got started with a not-so-scientific study that needs some smashing.

THE FRAUD THAT FUELED THE MODERN ANTI-VACCINE MOVEMENT

In 1998, an English medical journal called the *Lancet* published an article that suggested that the vaccine for measles, mumps, and rubella (MMR) caused autism, a developmental disorder, in children. This was understandably scary news for parents to read, and some decided not to have their kids vaccinated. But that claim wasn't true.

A few years later, the *British Medical Journal* discovered that the whole study had been "an elaborate fraud." The lead doctor who wrote it, Andrew Wakefield, had said the patients in his study were random kids admitted to the hospital where he worked, when really they had been referred to him by a lawyer for families trying to sue vaccine makers. Wakefield had been paid hundreds of thousands of dollars to do the study, which featured only a dozen children. The parents of those kids were convinced that the vaccine had caused the autism. But it turns out that the age kids are when they have the MMR vaccine just happens to be the age when autism symptoms usually show up. Before publishing his fraudulent article, Wakefield had patented what he said was a "safer" vaccine for measles. He could have made a lot of money on that if everyone abandoned the old vaccine.

But the fraud was uncovered. The *Lancet* retracted, or took back, the study, and Wakefield was banned from practicing medicine in the United Kingdom. But that didn't happen until 2010, and many people had already skipped the vaccine. In 2006 and 2007, there were more than twelve thousand new cases of measles in Europe.

Since the Wakefield article was debunked, dozens of studies involving millions of children have shown that vaccines do *not* cause autism. But the myth continues to spread, and a deadly illness is spreading along with it. Measles had been eliminated in the United States in 2000 but has made a roaring comeback because some people still believe that fake study. In 2019, the United States saw 1,282 cases of measles, its highest number since 1992.

In 2019, the World Health Organization listed vaccine hesitancy as one of ten major threats to global health, and misinformation about vaccines is still a problem. Even as the COVID-19 vaccines were being developed, people began spreading rumors about them that aren't true. Here's a look at a few of those fake news stories that need smashing.

THE RUMOR: mRNA vaccines are made of genetic material and can change your DNA.

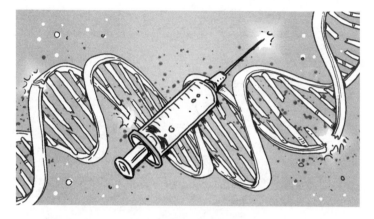

THE REALITY: mRNA vaccines don't have any effect on a person's DNA. The mRNA is simply a set of instructions so that your body can make the protein that causes it to produce antibodies. Once cells have made that protein, they break down the mRNA and get rid of it. It does not stay in the body.

THE RUMOR: Getting a vaccine can give you COVID-19.

THE REALITY: COVID-19 vaccines do not contain the virus and cannot give you the disease.

THE RUMOR: COVID-19 vaccines haven't been tested and are dangerous.

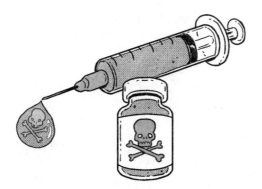

THE REALITY: COVID-19 vaccines are safe and effective. Those approved for emergency use have been tested on tens of thousands of volunteers and studied by teams of scientists who have determined that they are safe and very good at protecting people against infection.

There have even been false rumors that vaccines contain microchips or other types of technology that allow people to be tracked and spied on. This might be a fun plot for a made-up science-fiction movie, but it is not in any way true.

Spreading myths like these is harmful because doing so can make people afraid to get vaccines. That puts them in danger of getting sick and spreading illness to others. If you hear someone spreading misinformation about vaccines, you can help by sharing more reliable information from the CDC or WHO.

Even with vaccinations and modern science, microbes aren't going away anytime soon. Because infectious diseases are an ongoing threat, countries all over the world are cooperating, communicating, and collaborating more than ever. They're using an approach called One Health.

One Health is the idea that the health of people is connected to the health of animals and our shared environment.

When we protect **one**, we help protect **all**.

www.cdc.gov/onehealth

Veterinarians and other health care workers in Kenya work together to get a blood sample from a camel as part of a study in 2013.

Animals can be early warning signs that a disease is about to affect humans. Back when bubonic plague was spreading through Europe, people sometimes noticed dead rats around a town before an outbreak hit citizens who lived there. The same sort of thing still happens, with birds in an area dying of West Nile virus (which is carried by mosquitoes) before the disease appears in humans. More than half of all the diseases that affect people can be spread by animals, so the One Health approach involves sharing information between doctors, nurses, veterinarians, farmers, environmental experts, and government officials. If farmers notice a disease outbreak in their animals and report it, officials can investigate right away and maybe prevent that disease from spreading to people.

The CDC's One Health office works with countries all over the world. One project involved training farmers in Thailand to use an app to report diseases and deaths in animals, as an early warning system. Health officials recognize now that countries need to cooperate when it comes to preventing infectious diseases, since microbes don't pay any attention to borders.

One Health also relies on education. Public health workers share guidelines and best practices for farmers and pet owners to reduce the spread of disease. For farmers, that includes using antibiotics only according to best practices so that misuse doesn't lead to drug-resistant bacteria. For the rest of us, preventing the spread of disease means being smart about interactions with animals. Even backyard chickens and pet reptiles can carry dangerous microbes, so it's important to wash your hands well after handling any animals.

The other good news about fighting future diseases is that modern technology has made it easier for scientists to study them. When COVID-19 broke out in China, researchers sequenced the virus's genetic code before it spread. They shared that information with scientists all over the world so they could work together to learn more about it, develop treatments, and come up with vaccines.

Maybe you'll be one of those disease detectives one day. But for now, your job is a little easier—you can do your part to fight the spread of infectious diseases by following simple guidelines that can make a big difference.

Be careful not to spread fake news about diseases or vaccines. Always check the source before you share something online or when you wonder about a story someone else has shared.

When there's an outbreak: Follow the advice of scientists and health officials. You may be asked to keep a healthy distance from others and wear a mask when you're out in public.

Always: Wash your hands often. Make sure they're nice and sudsy, and scrub for at least twenty seconds, long enough to sing the "Happy Birthday" song twice!

AUTHOR'S NOTE

I was excited to write this installment in the History Smashers series for a few reasons. First, because I love science and have always been especially fascinated with epidemiology, the branch of science dedicated to the study of diseases. But also because this topic is a personal one for my family. When I was growing up, I remember hearing stories about how my grandmother on my dad's side had a very hard life.

Grandma Schirmer became an orphan when both of her parents died in the influenza pandemic of 1918. With nowhere to go, she went to work as a hired girl at a local inn when she was just eleven years old. I think about her when I get my flu shot every year, and I think about how the world has changed, thanks to science.

Delia Schirmer in an old family photo

But science hasn't solved everything. When I first started working on the History Smashers series, I couldn't have predicted that I would be drafting this sixth book in the middle of a pandemic. I couldn't have guessed that I'd need to leave half a chapter blank, waiting to add more details about how—and if—the outbreak would end.

Usually, I spend the school year visiting classrooms, but this year everything was canceled. Like most Americans, I've been staying home, and wearing a mask when I have to venture out to the grocery store. I've been watching the scientists on the news at night, feeling hopeful about the research they're doing but also frustrated that even after all the pandemics the world has experienced, some people still won't listen to those scientists. And because I've always been a curious person, I'm also feeling a sense of wonder at the way microbes work. It's pretty amazing that with all of our technological advances, something too small to see can still stop our entire society in its tracks.

More than anything, though, I'm feeling grateful for the scientists and public health experts who have been doing their best to lead our world through this crisis. That includes experts at the WHO, CDC, and NIH, as well as other researchers around the globe. They're our modern-day health care heroes, and I'm hopeful that by the time you read this book, their work will have us all in a better place. I'm also grateful to those who helped out with this book by serving as early readers and reviewers, including Ella Messner, Linda Urban, Dr. Loree Griffin Burns, and Justin Bevere, assistant director of the Vaccine Development Center of West Virginia University.

Here are some resources to explore if you'd like to learn more about pandemics and public health.

BOOKS

NONFICTION

All in a Drop: How Antony van Leeuwenhoek Discovered an Invisible World by Lori Alexander, illustrated by Vivien Mildenberger (HMH, 2019)

An American Plague: The True and Terrifying Story of the Yellow Fever Epidemic of 1793 by Jim Murphy (Clarion, 2003)

Bubonic Plague: How the Black Death Changed History by Barbara Krasner (Capstone, 2019)

Bugged: How Insects Changed History by Sarah Albee (Bloomsbury, 2014)

Do Not Lick This Book by Idan Ben-Barak, illustrated by Julian Frost (Roaring Brook Press, 2018)

Dr. Fauci: How a Boy from Brooklyn Became America's Doctor by Kate Messner, illustrated by Alexandra Bye (Simon & Schuster, 2021)

Dr. Jenner and the Speckled Monster: The Discovery of the Smallpox Vaccine by Albert Marrin (Dutton, 2002)

Ebola: Fears and Facts by Patricia Newman (Millbrook, 2016)

Fatal Fever: Tracking Down Typhoid Mary by Gail Jarrow (Calkins Creek, 2015)

Fever Year: The Killer Flu of 1918 by Don Brown (HMH, 2019)

Germs: Fact and Fiction, Friends and Foes by Lesa Cline-Ransom, illustrated by James Ransome (Henry Holt, 2017)

Germs Up Close by Sara Levine (Millbrook, 2021)

Invincible Microbe: Tuberculosis and the Never-Ending Search for a Cure by Jim Murphy and Alison Blank (Clarion, 2012)

Outbreak: 50 Tales of Epidemics That Terrorized the World by Beth Skwarecki (Simon & Schuster, 2016)

Outbreak! Plagues that Changed History by Bryn Barnard (Crown Books, 2005)

The Polio Pioneer by Linda Elovitz Marshall, illustrated by Lisa Anchin (Knopf, 2020)

Science Comics: Plagues: The Microscopic Battlefield by Falynn Koch (First Second, 2017)

The Secret of the Yellow Death: A True Story of Medical Sleuthing by Suzanne Jurmain (HMH, 2009)

A Shot in the Arm! (Big Ideas That Changed the World) by Don Brown (Amulet Books, 2021)

Smallpox: How a Pox Changed History by Jamie Havemeyer (Capstone, 2019)

Tiny Creatures: The World of Microbes by Nicola Davies, illustrated by Emily Sutton (Candlewick, 2016)

Very, Very, Very Dreadful: The Influenza Pandemic of 1918 by Albert Marrin (Knopf, 2018)

HISTORICAL FICTION

Chasing Secrets by Gennifer Choldenko (Random House, 2015)

Fever 1793 by Laurie Halse Anderson (Simon & Schuster, 2000)

The Great Trouble: A Mystery of London, the Blue Death, and a Boy Called Eel by Deborah Hopkinson (Knopf, 2013)

Winnie's War by Jenny Moss (Walker, 2009)

WEBSITES

"The Deadly Virus: The Influenza Epidemic of 1918" is an online exhibit from the National Archives, featuring a collection of documents and photographs from the pandemic. archives.gov /exhibits/influenza-epidemic

"Diseases & the Vaccines That Prevent Them" at the Centers for Disease Control and Prevention (CDC) website gives an excellent overview of vaccine-preventable illnesses. cdc.gov /healthyschools/bam/diseases/diseases_and_vaccines.htm

Doctors Without Borders works to fight disease all over the world, especially in poor nations. You can read about the organization and make a donation if your family or school would like to hold a fundraiser to help the group's efforts. blogs.msf.org

The History of Vaccines, a website from the College of Physicians of Philadelphia, has several interesting interactive resources.

"How Vaccines Work": historyofvaccines.org/content/how-vaccines-work

"The Scientific Method": historyofvaccines.org/content/scientific-method

"A Timeline of Diseases and Vaccines in History": historyofvaccines.org/timeline/all

"The Most Dangerous Woman in America" from PBS's NOVA tells the story of Typhoid Mary, complete with a timeline and a letter from Mary. pbs.org/wgbh/nova/typhoid

"Solve the Outbreak," a game at the CDC website, lets you become a disease detective. cdc.gov/mobile/applications/sto/web-app.html

The World Health Organization website has an informative page about safe drinking water and its importance to health. who.int/news-room/fact-sheets/detail/drinking-water

GLOSSARY

ANTIBIOTIC—a drug that slows the growth of or kills bacteria and is used to treat bacterial infections

ANTIBIOTIC RESISTANCE—the ability of some bacteria to avoid being harmed or killed by antibiotics. Antibiotic resistance can make bacterial diseases difficult to treat.

ANTIBODY—a protein that attaches to a specific invader in the body, such as a bacterium or virus, to help weaken or kill it

BACTERIUM—a type of one-celled organism that can sometimes cause disease (plural: *bacteria*)

DNA (short for *deoxyribonucleic acid*)—a double-stranded molecule found in the cells of living things and in some viruses that determines the characteristics of an organism or a virus

EPIDEMIC—an outbreak of a disease that spreads quickly and affects many people within an area at the same time

MICROBE—a tiny living thing that can be seen only with a microscope

MUTATION—a change in a microbe's genetic material that can cause vaccines to be less effective

PANDEMIC—an outbreak of a disease that affects a very large number of people in a wide area, sometimes the entire world

PARASITE—an organism that survives by living in or on a host organism while usually causing disease or other harm to the host

QUARANTINE—a period of isolation by someone who has been infected with or exposed to a disease, in order to avoid spreading the illness to others

R0—the average number of people to whom each person infected in an outbreak spreads the disease

RNA (short for *ribonucleic acid*)—a single-stranded molecule found in cells and in some viruses that helps determine the characteristics of an organism or a virus. RNA is similar to DNA but has a slightly different structure.

STRAIN—a group of microbes that are genetically distinct from others within the same species. Different strains may behave differently and require different vaccines for protection.

SUPER-SPREADER—an infected person who spreads disease to an unusually large number of other people

VACCINATION—a process that helps people gain immunity to a disease, often by exposing them to a weakened or killed form of the microbe that causes the disease

VIRUS—a bit of genetic information surrounded by a protein coat that reproduces by infecting cells. Viruses can sometimes cause disease.

SELECTED BIBLIOGRAPHY

Ackerknecht, Erwin H. *History and Geography of the Most Important Diseases*. New York: Hafner, 1965.

Anti-Defamation League. "Reports of Anti-Asian Assaults, Harassment, and Hate Crimes Rise as Coronavirus Spreads." Accessed May 27, 2020. adl.org/blog/reports-of-anti-asian -assaults-harassment-and-hate-crimes-rise-as-coronavirus -spreads.

Baron, John. *The Life of Edward Jenner M.D.* London: Henry Colburn, 1838.

Boseley, Sarah. "How Disgraced Anti-vaxxer Andrew Wakefield Was Embraced by Trump's America." *The Guardian*, July 18, 2018. theguardian.com/society/2018/jul/18/how-disgraced-anti -vaxxer-andrew-wakefield-was-embraced-by-trumps-america.

Branswell, Helen. "History Credits This Man with Discovering Ebola on His Own. History Is Wrong." STAT, July 14, 2016. statnews .com/2016/07/14/history-ebola-peter-piot.

Brink, Susan. "What's the Real Story About the Milkmaid and the Smallpox Vaccine?" NPR, February 1, 2018. npr.org/sections /goatsandsoda/2018/02/01/582370199/whats-the-real-story -about-the-milkmaid-and-the-smallpox-vaccine.

Caulford, Paul. "SARS: Aftermath of an Outbreak." Supplement, *Lancet* 362 (2003): s2—s3. https://doi.org/10.1016/S0140 -6736(03)15052-0.

Centers for Disease Control and Prevention. "2014–2016 Ebola Outbreak in West Africa." Accessed June 30, 2020. cdc.gov/vhf /ebola/history/2014-2016-outbreak/index.html.

Centers for Disease Control and Prevention. "One Health." May 22, 2020. cdc.gov/onehealth/index.html.

Centers for Disease Control and Prevention. "Progress Toward Global Eradication of Poliomyelitis, January 2003—April 2004." *MMWR* 53 (June 25, 2004): 343–346. cdc.gov/mmwr/preview /mmwrhtml/mm5324a5.htm.

Centers for Disease Control and Prevention. "Understanding How Vaccines Work." Updated July 2018. cdc.gov/vaccines/hcp /conversations/downloads/vacsafe-understand-color-office.pdf.

Cockburn, Aidan. *The Evolution and Eradication of Infectious Diseases.* Baltimore: Johns Hopkins University Press, 1963.

Cohn, Samuel K. "Pandemics: Waves of Disease, Waves of Hate from the Plague of Athens to AIDS." *Historical Journal* (Cambridge, England) 85, no. 230 (November 1, 2012): 535–555. ncbi.nlm.nih .gov/pmc/articles/PMC4422154.

Crawford, Dorothy H. *Deadly Companions: How Microbes Shaped Our History.* Oxford: Oxford University Press, 2007.

Crosby, Alfred W. *The Columbian Exchange: Biological and Cultural Consequences of 1492.* Westport, CT: Greenwood, 1972.

Cunha, Burke A. "The Cause of the Plague of Athens: Plague, Typhoid, Typhus, Smallpox, or Measles?" *Infectious Disease Clinics of North America* 18, no. 1 (March 2004): 29–43. https://doi.org/10.1016 /S0891-5520(03)00100-4.

Daniels, T. M. "The Impact of Tuberculosis on Civilization." *Infectious Disease Clinics of North America* 18, no. 1 (March 2004): 157–165. https://doi.org/10.1016/S0891-5520(03)00096-5.

Dillard, Coshandra. "Speaking Up Against Racism Around the New Coronavirus." *Teaching Tolerance,* February 14, 2020. tolerance .org/magazine/speaking-up-against-racism-around-the-new -coronavirus.

Dinc, Gulten, and Yesim Isil Ulman. "The Introduction of Variolation 'A La Turca' to the West by Lady Mary Montagu and Turkey's Contribution to This." *Vaccine* 25, no. 21 (May 22, 2007): 4261–4265. https://doi.org/10.1016/j.vaccine.2007.02.076.

Ellis, Rebecca. "CHART: Where Mosquito-Carrying Mosquitoes Will Go in the Future." NPR, March 28, 2019. npr.org/sections /goatsandsoda/2019/03/28/707604928/chart-where-disease -carrying-mosquitoes-will-go-in-the-future.

Ewald, Paul W. *Evolution of Infectious Disease.* Oxford: Oxford University Press, 1994.

Fauci, Anthony. Zoom interview with the author, November 23, 2020.

Gaynes, Robert P. *Germ Theory: Medical Pioneers in Infectious Diseases.* Washington, DC: ASM Press, 2011.

Gellene, Denise. "Overlooked No More: June Almeida, Scientist Who Identified the First Coronavirus." *New York Times,* May 8, 2020. nytimes.com/2020/05/08/obituaries/june-almeida-overlooked -coronavirus.html.

Gill, Victoria. "Black Death 'Spread by Humans Not Rats.'" *BBC News,* January 15, 2018. bbc.com/news/science-environment-42690577.

Girard, Philippe R. "Napoleon Bonaparte and the Emancipation Issue in Saint-Domingue, 1799–1803." *French Historical Studies* 32, no. 4 (Fall 2009): 587–618.

Girard, Philippe R. *The Slaves Who Defeated Napoleon.* Tuscaloosa: University of Alabama Press, 2011.

Global Polio Eradication Initiative. "Afghanistan." Accessed June 29, 2020. polioeradication.org/where-we-work/afghanistan.

Global Polio Eradication Initiative. "Pakistan." Accessed June 29, 2020. polioeradication.org/where-we-work/pakistan.

Goetz, Thomas. *The Remedy: Robert Koch, Arthur Conan Doyle, and the Quest to Cure Tuberculosis.* New York: Gotham Books, 2014.

Grady, Denise. "Not His First Epidemic: Dr. Anthony Fauci Sticks to the Facts." *New York Times,* March 8, 2020. nytimes .com/2020/03/08/health/fauci-coronavirus .html?searchResultPosition=1.

"The Great Fever Plot." *New York Times,* May 26, 1865. nytimes. com/1865/05/26/archives/the-great-fever-plot-examination -of-the-notorious-dr-blackburn-at.html.

Greenfieldboyce, Nell. "Inside a Secret Government Warehouse Prepped for Health Catastrophes." NPR, June 27, 2016. npr.org /sections/health-shots/2016/06/27/483069862/inside-a-secret -government-warehouse-prepped-for-health-catastrophes.

Greshko, Michael. "Maybe Rats Aren't to Blame for the Black Death." *National Geographic,* January 15, 2018. nationalgeographic.com /news/2018/01/rats-plague-black-death-humans-lice-health -science/#close.

Henkel, John. "Attacking AIDS with a 'Cocktail' Therapy: Drug Combo Sends Deaths Plummeting." *FDA Consumer,* July–August 1999.

Hewings-Martin, Yella. "How Do SARS and MERS Compare with COVID-19?" *Medical News Today,* April 10, 2020. medicalnewstoday.com/articles/how-do-sars-and-mers -compare-with-covid-19.

HIV.gov. "Global HIV/AIDS Overview." United States Department of Health and Human Services. Updated July 7, 2020. hiv.gov /federal-response/pepfar-global-aids/global-hiv-aids-overview.

Jones, Absalom, and Richard Allen. *A Narrative of the Proceedings of the Black People, During the Late Awful Calamity in Philadelphia, in the Year 1793.* Philadelphia: William W. Woodward, 1794.

Kelly, John. *The Great Mortality: An Intimate History of the Black Death, the Most Devastating Plague of All Time.* New York: HarperCollins, 2005.

Kolata, Gina. *Flu: The Story of the Great Influenza Pandemic of 1918 and the Search for the Virus that Caused It.* New York: Atria, 1999.

Kota, S. L., and J. E. Jessler. *Yellow Fever: A Worldwide History.* Jefferson, NC: McFarland, 2017.

Langfitt, Frank. "Boris Johnson Released from London Hospital." NPR, April 12, 2020. npr.org/sections/coronavirus-live -updates/2020/04/12/832772094/boris-johnson-released-from -london-hospital.

Li, Wendong, et al. "Bats Are Natural Reservoirs of SARS-like Coronaviruses." *Science* 310, no. 5748 (October 28, 2005): 676–679.

Mailman, Erika. "In 1919, the Mayor of Oakland Was Arrested for Failing to Wear a Mask." *Smithsonian,* May 21, 2020. smithsonianmag.com/history/when-mayor-oakland-was -arrested-failing-wear-mask-180974950.

Markel, Howard. *When Germs Travel: Six Major Epidemics That Have Invaded America Since 1900 and the Fears They Have Unleashed.* New York: Pantheon Books, 2004.

Marr, John S., and John T. Cathey. "The 1802 Saint-Domingue Yellow Fever Epidemic and the Louisiana Purchase." *Journal of Public Health Management and Practice* 19, no. 1 (2013): 77–82.

McLean, Angela, Robert M. May, John Pattison, and Robin A. Weiss. *SARS: A Case Study in Emerging Infections.* Oxford: Oxford University Press, 2005.

McNeill, J. R. *Mosquito Empires: Ecology and War in the Greater Caribbean, 1620–1914.* Cambridge: Cambridge University Press, 2010.

McNeill, William H. *Plagues and Peoples.* New York: Random House, 1976.

Minard, Anne. "Spawn of Medieval 'Black Death' Bug Still Roam the Earth." *National Geographic,* October 13, 2011. nationalgeographic.com/news/2011/10/111012-plague-black -death-yersinia-pestis-genetics-nature-health.

Oldstone, Michael. *Viruses, Plagues, & History: Past, Present, and Future.* Oxford: Oxford University Press, 2010.

Oshinky, David M. *Polio: An American Story.* Oxford: Oxford University Press, 2005.

Pallardy, Richard. "Larry Kramer." In *Encyclopaedia Britannica.* Encyclopaedia Britannica, Inc., June 21, 2020. britannica.com /biography/Larry-Kramer.

Peralta, Eyder. "This Congolese Doctor Discovered Ebola But Never Got Credit for It—Until Now." NPR, November 4, 2019. npr.org /sections/goatsandsoda/2019/11/04/774863495/this-congolese -doctor-discovered-ebola-but-never-got-credit-for-it-until-now.

Person, Bobbie, et al. "Fear and Stigma: The Epidemic Within the SARS Outbreak." *Emerging Infectious Diseases* 10, no. 2 (2004): 358–363. ncbi.nlm.nih.gov/pmc/articles/PMC3322940.

Powell, J. H. *Bring Out Your Dead: The Great Plague of the Yellow Fever in Philadelphia in 1793.* Philadelphia: University of Pennsylvania Press, 1993. First published 1949.

Procopius. *History of the Wars.* Vol. 1. Translated by H. B. Dewing. Cambridge, MA: Harvard University Press, 1914.

Quammen, David. *Spillover: Animal Infections and the Next Human Pandemic.* New York: W. W. Norton, 2012.

Quick, Jonathan D., and Heidi Larson. "The Vaccine-Autism Myth Started 20 Years Ago. Here's Why It Still Endures Today." *Time,* February 28, 2018. time.com/5175704/andrew-wakefield-vaccine -autism.

Riedel, Stefan. "Edward Jenner and the History of Smallpox and Vaccination." *Baylor University Medical Center Proceedings* 18, no. 1 (2005): 21–25. https://doi.org/10.1080/08998280.2005.11928028.

Robson, David. "Why Smart People Believe Coronavirus Myths." *BBC Future,* April 6, 2020. bbc.com/future/article/20200406-why -smart-people-believe-coronavirus-myths.

Rogers, Naomi. *Polio Wars: Sister Kenny and the Golden Age of American Medicine.* New York: Oxford University Press, 2014.

Runlet, Philip. "The British, the Indians, and Smallpox: What Actually Happened at Fort Pitt in 1763?" *Pennsylvania History: A Journal of Mid-Atlantic Studies,* 67, no. 3 (2000): 427–441. Accessed June 16, 2020. http://www.jstor.com/stable/27774278.

Sanderson, A. T., and Edmund Tapp. "Disease in Ancient Egypt." In *Mummies, Diseases, and Ancient Cultures,* edited by Aidan Cockburn, Eve Cockburn, Theodore A. Reyman. 2nd ed. Cambridge: Cambridge University Press, 1998.

Schwarz, Hans Peter, and Friedrich Dorner. "Karl Landsteiner and His Major Contributions to Haematology." *British Journal of Haematology* 121, no. 4 (May 2003): 556–565. https://doi .org/10.1046/j.1365-2141.2003.04295.x.

Semenza, Jan C. "Cascading Risks of Waterborne Diseases from Climate Change." *Nature Immunology* 21, no. 5 (May 2020): 479–487. https://doi.org/10.1038/s41590-020-0631-7.

Serhan, Yasmeen, and Timothy McLaughlin. "The Other Problematic Outbreak." *Atlantic*, March 13, 2020. theatlantic.com /international/archive/2020/03/coronavirus-covid19 -xenophobia-racism/607816.

Shilts, Randy. *And the Band Played On: Politics, People, and the AIDS Epidemic*. New York: St. Martin's, 1987.

Snowden, Frank. *Epidemics and Society: From the Black Death to the Present*. New Haven: Yale University Press, 2019.

Spinney, Laura. *Pale Rider: The Spanish Flu of 1918 and How It Changed the World*. New York: PublicAffairs, 2017.

Stanbridge, Nicola. "DNA Confirms Cause of 1665 London's Great Plague." *BBC News*, September 8, 2016. bbc.com/news/science -environment-37287715.

Taylor, Derrick Bryson. "A Timeline of the Coronavirus Pandemic." *New York Times*, August 6, 2020. nytimes.com/article /coronavirus-timeline.html.

Thucydides. *The History of the Peloponnesian War*. Auckland, New Zealand: The Floating Press, 1874.

US Department of Defense. *Addressing Emerging Infectious Disease Threats: A Strategic Plan for the Department of Defense*. Washington, DC: US Government Printing Office, 1998.

US Department of Health and Human Services. "Stockpile Responses." Public Health Emergency. Last updated December 17, 2020. phe.gov/about/sns/Pages/responses.aspx.

US Department of Health and Human Services. "Vaccines Protect Your Community." Last reviewed February 2020. vaccines.gov /basics/work/protection.

Watts, Sheldon. *Epidemics and History*. New Haven, CT: Yale University Press, 1997.

Wee, Sui-Lee, and Donald G. McNeil. "China Identifies New Virus Causing Pneumonialike Illness." *New York Times,* January 8, 2020. nytimes.com/2020/01/08/health/china-pneumonia-outbreak -virus.html.

Wheelis, Mark. "Biological Warfare at the 1346 Siege of Caffa." *Emerging Infectious Diseases* 8, no. 9 (September 2002): 971–975. dx.doi.org/10.3201/eid0809.010536.

Wilford, John Noble. "Malaria Is a Likely Killer in King Tut's Post-Mortem." *New York Times,* February 16, 2010. nytimes .com/2010/02/17/science/17tut.html.

Wolfe, Nathan. *The Viral Storm: The Dawn of a New Pandemic Age.* New York: St. Martin's, 2011.

World Health Organization. "Climate Change and Human Health." who.int/globalchange/summary/en/index5.html.

World Health Organization. "How Do Vaccines Work?" Accessed December 6, 2020. who.int/emergencies/diseases/novel -coronavirus-2019/covid-19-vaccines/how-do-vaccines-work.

World Health Organization. "Update 49—SARS Case Fatality Ratio, Incubation Period." May 7, 2003. who.int/csr/sars /archive/2003_05_07a/en.

Wyns, Arthur. "Climate Change and Infectious Diseases." *Scientific American,* April 9, 2020. blogs.scientificamerican.com /observations/climate-change-and-infectious-diseases.

"Yellow Fever Epidemic of 1853 in New Orleans." *American Journal of the Medical Sciences* 26, no. 52 (1853): 551–554.

IMAGE CREDITS

INDEX

HISTORY SMASHERS

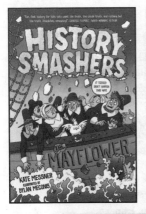